SECRETS OF WINNING VIDEO POKER

ABOUT THE AUTHOR

Avery Cardoza is the foremost gambling authority in the world and best-selling author of twenty-one gambling books and advanced strategies, including *How to Win at Gambling, Secrets of Winning Slots*, and the classic, *Winning Casino Blackjack for the Non-Counter*.

Cardoza began his gambling career underage in Las Vegas as a professional blackjack player beating the casinos at their own game and was soon barred from one casino after another. In 1981, when even the biggest casinos refused him play, Cardoza founded Cardoza Publishing, which has sold more than five million books and published close to 100 gaming titles.

Though originally from Brooklyn, New York, where he is occasionally found, Cardoza has used his winnings to pursue a lifestyle of extensive traveling in exotic locales around the world.

In 1994, he established Cardoza Entertainment, a multimedia development and publishing house, to produce interactive gambling simulations that give players a taste of a real casino with animated and responsive dealers, and the full scale of bets at the correct odds. The result, *Avery Cardoza's Casino*, featuring 65 gambling variations, became an instant entertainment hit making its way onto USA Today's best-seller's list. It also catapulted Cardoza Entertainment, measured by average sales per title, as the number two seller of games in the entire industry for the first six months of 1997, ahead of such giants as Dreamworks, Microsoft, and others. Their second title, *Avery Cardoza's 100 Slots*, was a simulated slots palace with 101 machines, and became another best-seller.

Cardoza's latest project, Avery Cardoza's *PLAYER*, a new gambling lifestyle magazine, will hit newsstands nationwide in the Fall of 2003.

SECRETS OF WINNING VIDEO POKER

Avery Cardoza

CARDOZA PUBLISHING

SECOND EDITION

Library of Congress Catalog No: 2003100601
ISBN: 1-58042-106-7

TABLE OF CONTENTS

SECTION A: THE BASICS

SECTION B: VIDEO POKER VARIETIES

SECTION A
- THE BASICS -

1. INTRODUCTION

There's a big reason for video poker's increasing popularity – if you play properly, you can actually have an edge over the casino. Like with blackjack, you can expect to win money every time you play!

That's right. With proper strategy, you'll have the edge against certain video poker machines, and against others, you can bring the house edge down to the barest minimum. There are still other video poker machines that give the house a whopping edge, and these will drain your bankroll quickly. In this book, I'll show you not only how to identify the great, the good, and the bad machines, but also the proper strategies to get the best possible chances of winning.

We'll cover all the basics of playing and winning with a focus on the practical aspects of winning so that anyone can use the strategies under actual casino conditions. Rather than provide you with an overwhelming detail-oriented strategy, I'll show you a practical approach that concentrates on the essentials.

This simplified, optimal strategy sacrifices mere tenths of

one percent. It allows you to play not only more mistake-free (and ultimately more accurately and profitably), but also faster and more easily, so you'll enjoy more relaxation and fun.

At the same time, I'm going to show you how to take advantage of all the benefits casinos are willing to bestow on their good video poker players through the use of the Slots Clubs. You'll get free rooms, comp buffets and meals, line passes to move you ahead of other patrons at long lines, discounted or free show tickets to the best spectaculars in town, and much more.

This book is about winning and taking the casino's money if you play smart. It's also about having a great time at the casinos while giving yourself the best chances of beating the machines. Can you actually beat the video poker machines? Yes, you can, but only if you know how to put the odds on your side.

That's what we're going to do with this book. Now let's take a closer look and see how we can beat the casino at video poker!

2. BASICS OF PLAY

Playing a video machine is quite easy. It's literally no more complicated than putting coins in the machine itself and pressing the "DEAL" button. This triggers the machine to deal five cards from which you will make a strategy decision. We'll cover the proper strategies for each of the machines later. Meanwhile, let's just look at the basics of play and the general information you need to know to get set up to play at the machines.

OBJECT OF THE GAME

Your goal in video poker is to achieve the winning poker combinations listed on the front of the machine so that you earn coins and credits. The higher the poker hand is ranked (as listed), the greater the payout will be.

For many players, the real goal in video poker is to hit the royal flush, especially if they're playing on a big progressive jackpot. Certainly hitting the royal flush is desirable for all video poker players.

HOW TO PLAY

Video poker is basically played as draw poker. The typical game employs a 52-card deck, which is dealt fresh after each hand. While you won't receive the same card within a play – the machine will deal cards from the 52-card computer pack – the memory ends there. The deck is "reshuffled" after each deal.

There are video poker variations that use multiple decks and extra cards such as wild cards, but the principles are the same. We will discuss the particulars of those variations separately. Meanwhile, let's just look at the typical machines and how they're played. We'll save discussions on the other video poker varieties for when we get to them.

To start, you need to insert anywhere from one to five coins into the machine. The choice is yours – play one or play five at your discretion. (In later chapters I'll make recommendations about how many coins you should play.)

If you insert five coins, the machine will automatically deal a hand to you. However, if you insert fewer than five coins, you'll need to press the button marked **DRAW/DEAL** to receive your cards.

Five cards will show on the screen. These are your cards. You may keep one, some, all, or none of the cards. It's your decision. To keep a card, press the button marked **"HOLD"** underneath the card you wish to keep. There will be five hold buttons, one for each card. For each card you want to keep, you must press the hold button.

"HELD" will appear on the screen underneath each card or cards so chosen. The other cards (the ones you wish to discard) will not be kept by the machine.

THE BASICS OF PLAY

What happens if you press the wrong hold button by accident or change your mind? No problem. Press the corresponding button again. If the card indicated "HELD," it will no longer do so and will not be held by the computer. If you change your mind, press the button one more time, and again the "HELD" sign will come on the screen indicating that the card will be kept on the draw. Until you press the draw button, it is not too late to change your strategy decision.

A player may keep all five original cards, and he does so by pushing the hold button under each card. He may also discard all five original cards if he so desires. This is done by pressing the DRAW/DEAL button without having pressed any of the hold buttons.

Once you've decided how many cards to hold, you press the DRAW/DEAL button to receive some new cards. The "HELD" cards will remain, and those cards not chosen to be held will be replaced with new ones. This set of cards is the final hand.

If your hand is a winner, the machine will flash "**WINNER**" at the bottom of the screen. Winning hands are automatically paid according to the payoffs shown on the machine.

CREDIT

There is a useful feature offered on all video poker machines that allows you to play on winnings using a credit function built in to the machines. Let's say, for example, that you've just hit a win for twenty coins. Two things will

15

now happen.

First, you'll see "Credit - 20" appear on the machine. To continue playing without cashing out and reinserting coins, you can now press another button that will have lit up and be indicated by the label **Maximum Bet**, **Bet 5** or some similar name. This allows you to play five of your twenty credits toward a new hand. Your new hand will appear on the screen along with the information that your credit now stands at "15."

The second thing that will happen after your 20-coin win is that a button called the **Cashout** or **Payout** button will light up. If you press that button, the machine will give immediate payment of the winnings registered in the credit area.

The Cashout button can be used after any hand is completed to cash out wins that have accumulated. If you want to continue playing on credit and you're planning to play five coins, keep pressing the Maximum Bet button to get new hands dealt.

WINNING VIDEO POKER HANDS

Let's go over the winning hands in video poker. Then I'll show the payoffs you'll most likely encounter in the different games available.

The hands in the chart below are listed in ascending order, from weakest to strongest, with the exception of the five-of-a-kind hand, which is usually stronger than a royal flush composed of wild cards but weaker than the royal made naturally (without wild cards).

Typically, the minimum winning hand in video poker is jacks or better, though that varies by machine type. For example, Deuces Wild machines require at least a three-of-a-kind for a payout. Some forms of video poker will pay out winners on lesser combinations than jacks. For example, the Pick Five machines pay out for hands as low as a pair of 6s.

We'll start our overview of the types of hands that can be winners by looking at the low pairs payout (found only on specialty machines).

Specified Low Pairs – Two cards of equal value are called a pair. Machines may sometimes give payouts if you hold a hand less than jacks or better (the standard minimum hand on many machines). For example, there may be a payout for holding a pair of 6s-10s, as in the Pick Five game. This means a hand with any two equal cards between 6 and 10 would be a winner. The illustration below shows a pair of 6s.

Jacks or Better – Jacks or better refers to a pair of jacks, queens, kings, or aces.

Aces-Kings – Two aces or two kings.

Two Pair – Two sets of paired cards, such as K K and 10 10.

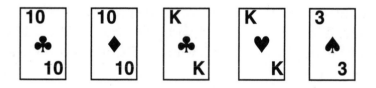

Three-of-a-kind – Three cards of equal value, such as 9 9 9.

Straight – Five cards in numerical sequence, such as 3 4 5 6 7 or 10 J Q K A. The ace can be counted as the highest card or the lowest card in a straight, however, it may not be in the middle of a five card run. Q K A 2 3, for example, is not a straight.

Flush – Any five cards of the same suit, such as five hearts.

Full House – Three-of-a-kind and a pair, such as 2 2 2 J J.

Four-of-a-kind – Four cards of equal value, such as K K K K.

Straight Flush – A straight all in the same suit, such as 7 8 9 10 J, all in spades.

Royal Flush (Wild) – 10 J Q K A, all in the same suit, with any of the cards substituted by a wild card. For example, in Deuces Wild, 10 J 2 K A is a royal flush (using the deuce to make the queen).

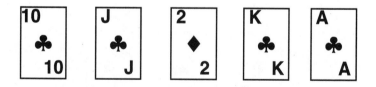

THE BASICS OF PLAY

Royal Flush – 10 J Q K A, all in the same suit. In wild card games, this type of royal would be called a "natural" royal flush, since no wild cards are used to make a royal.

Royal Flush (Sequential) – 10-J-Q-K-A, all in the same suit, however, with a sequential royal, all the cards must be in a particular order in position as specified by the machine. For example, 10 J Q K A might be specified in that order, or a reverse royal in the order of A K Q J 10, with no card, in either example, being out of sequence. Below is a sequential royal flush, A-K, in spades.

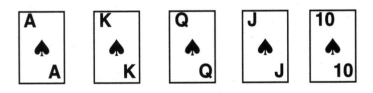

Five-of-a-kind - Five cards of equal value – a hand that's possible only in wild card video poker. For example, if deuces are wild, the hand 2 2 7 7 7 would be five 7s.

Five Wild Cards – 2-2-2-2-Joker in Deuces-Joker Wild would be even harder to draw than a royal flush. This hand is possible only in a game that has at least five wild cards.

3. CASINO BASICS

COIN DENOMINATIONS

Video Poker machines come in a variety of coin denominations, enough choice to meet any player's need. You can play the **small coin** machines, 5¢ and 25¢; the **medium coin** $1 machines; the **big coin** machines, $5 and $25; or the **high roller** versions, $100 or $500 per coin!! You saw it right. There are $100 and $500 coin machines in casinos. They cater to high rollers, and they do get action.

CONVERTING COINS INTO DOLLARS

When you've finished playing and are ready to convert your coins into bills, you'll need to make your way over to the change booth set up in the video poker or slots area. In the booth are wonderful machines that automatically sort and count your coins. The changeperson within simply takes your bucket, empties it upside down over the machine, and abracadabra! A few seconds later, the machine has counted up your total. That amount will be paid back to you by the cheerful changeperson in whatever denominations you please. (Changepeople can be cheerful; it's not their money.)

SECRETS OF WINNING VIDEO POKER

Note that the cashier's cage in the back is not typically set up to change coins. If you bring your bucket there, the cashier will just refer you back to the change booth in the slots area. If there is no change booth, however, then the cashier's cage will serve as both cage and change booth.

PLAYING THE MACHINES
Playing by Coin
Every video poker machine will have a coin slot, called a **coin entry**, or **coin acceptor**. The coin entry is where you insert your coins into the machine to initiate action. On the typical machine, you can put in anywhere from one coin to five coins to initiate play. If you try to put more than five coins in the machine, it will immediately return the extra coins back into the coin tray. For example, if six coins were placed into a machine, the extra coin would drop out of the bottom to be returned to the player.

Playing by Credits
Standard machines now all have bill changers that accept $1, $5, $20, $50 and even $100 bills. These bills get converted directly into credits on the machine. Later, you can convert these to coins, if you want, by pressing the CASH OUT button on the machine.

Once you have credits, spinning the reels at slots is as easy as could be. On every machine, you'll see a button marked "PLAY MAX COINS," "PLAY FIVE COINS," or something similar indicating that you can use your credits to play. You'll typically find this button on the right side of the machine near the coin acceptor, the area of the machine most convenient for easy play. You can expect this button to be large and easily visible.

Pressing this button automatically deals the cards if you have credits available. Experienced players use this button as if it were a speed dial. Press, result, press, result, press, result. They'll run through hands like a car racer navigating a speedway. Serious players love the credit button for its ease of play and speed. You'll find it a great feature, too.

If no credits are available, pressing this button won't activate anything. Only money walks. To get things going again, you'll need to deposit more coins into the coin slot or slide another bill into the hungry machine.

Establishing Credits
There are two ways to establish credits at a machine. The basic way of building credits is simply to put coins in the machine. Once coins are in, you can play. With the new bill acceptors inserted into the latest versions of machines, you can immediately establish credits by inserting a $20 or $100 bill, for example, into the machine. These credits will register on the display of the machine marked "Credits."

The second way to keep playing is to earn these credits through wins. After every win, the amount won automatically gets credited to your total. This amount will be posted underneath the area marked "credits." For example, if you win twenty credits, the number "20" will be posted to your credits. If you already had fifty credits accrued, then the win of twenty would bump that total up to "70."

You can play on these credits as long as you have them or

cash out at any time by pressing the "CASH OUT" button. Pressing the CASH OUT button will release the coins into the drop slot below. When you win a lot of coins, you'll hear a loud thunder of coins dropping, a commotion sure to raise the excitement level of all players within earshot of this winning hullabaloo.

If you win more coins than the machine will pay out, an attendant will come by to pay the rest or get a manager to authorize that payment. Usually, the maximum number of coins that the machine will pay for winners is posted right on the machine itself. It will also state that the attendant will pay the remainder. If that is the case, do not leave your machine if you hit a big winner – always wait until the attendant arrives to give you your winnings.

TIP

Never, ever leave a machine that owes you money. Wait for the attendants to come by, no matter how long it takes.

The casinos love players who play on credits and encourage as many of them as they can to do so. Why? The reason is simple. Players who play on credits play at a speed many multiples faster than those who are fishing around for coins to get every play started. The faster the machines are played, the more bets end up being played per hour. And that translates directly into more profits for the casinos against players who are not armed with winning strategies.

On the other hand, more hands per hour also adds up to more profits for the prepared player.

THE VIDEO POKER ENVIRONMENT

You walk into the casino, hot cash in hand, and say to yourself, "I come to gamble." The casino is buzzing with noise and excitement, and a hum of voices gathers and hangs in the air. Over by the craps table a Texan is screaming, "Eighter from Decatur!" You don't understand craps anyway. The blackjack tables are quieter but don't look inviting, and roulette just isn't your style.

Forget all that. You came to play video poker. So let's talk about what the video poker environment looks and feels like.

The Video Poker Setting

Video Poker machines are situated together in groups called **banks**. A bank of machines might consist of four machines grouped together in a squarish shape, with backs toward the middle and fronts facing outward towards the players. It could also be a larger group of eight, ten, fifteen, or even more machines, in a circular or rectangular formation.

Unlike slot machines, where there are often a variety of machines grouped together in the same bank, video poker machines tend to be grouped together by similar types. For example, Deuces Wild machines will tend to be side-by-side on the floor, as will the Jacks or Better versions.

A bank of video poker machines will almost always contain machines using the same coin denomination. It is unusual to see different denominations (such as 25¢ and $1) of machines mixed together within the same bank. This type of arrangement makes it easier for customers to identify the type and denomination of machines they want to play.

Progressive video poker machines are typically "banked" together in the same block, and at the equal coin value, so that the posted sign showing the progressive jackpot above the machines can refer to all the machines within the group. Banks of progressives are common in a casino. They're great draws for most players.

Chairs

Each video poker machine in the casino has a chair in front of it so that you can play the machines in comfort, even if you were to play for hours, as many of the players do.

Plastic Buckets

Throughout the video poker area, between the machines, sometimes on top or at the ends of aisles, you'll find plastic buckets. They look like small ice buckets emblazoned with the name and logo of the casino, but it's not cold cubes they're meant to hold. It's coins – bucketfuls of them.

Players use these plastic buckets to hold their coins after cashing out from a machine so that they can transport their haul over to the cashier's cage. You'll often see players scooping coins out of the coin well and shoveling them into their buckets prior to leaving the machine. Some players will use the buckets while they play as well – they're a convenient way to hold multiple coins.

CASINO BASICS

VIDEO POKER EMPLOYEES

The casino has a number of staff devoted to the video poker and slots areas. Let's take a moment to go over their functions.

Changepeople

You can't help but notice the number of changepeople constantly on patrol through the slots area, even in smaller casinos. The main job of these employees is to provide coins or tokens readily for any player who needs them. A secondary job of these "front line" employees is to keep the players happy, whether through commiserating if they hit a losing streak, exchanging small talk, or giving hints that a player might request.

Casinos are well aware that a moment's hesitation in getting a customer his or her change could cause that player to get bored or annoyed and leave the area, so they've kept the area well-stocked with changepeople. It is not unusual to see two or even three changepeople patrolling a section.

Waitpeople

Playing video poker is supposed to be fun, and to make sure you agree with the casino on this issue, they keep you well stocked with drinks while you play. You have a full choice of the drinks available, from coffee, tea, milk and sodas, to beer, wine, shots and mixed drinks. In smoking sections, you can also request cigarettes if you're a smoker. And all this is without charge.

However, just like at any place that serves drinks, such as a bar, it is customary to tip the server 50¢ or a dollar, perhaps more if you've ordered a bunch of drinks or if a big-time win has you feeling large.

Slots Hosts

Most major casinos (and many smaller ones), have hired an employee specifically assigned to take care of the slots and video poker players' needs. This employee, called the slots host, often works out of a booth set aside for these players. The booth may have a placard that says "Slots Host" or "Casino Host."

The slots hosts spend much of their time working with slots club members, issuing new cards and memberships, processing special requests, or dealing with issues that come up. Their job is to take good care of the slots and video poker players and to make sure that their experiences at the casino are as first rate as they can make them.

TIPPING

Just as in the table games (and many service industries), tipping is sort of an expected service in casinos. There are several employees you may want to tip. First of all, as I've mentioned, you have the waitpeople bringing you drinks. It is customary to tip them every time they bring you a drink or round of drinks. One dollar or 50¢ will generally do, unless you order a bunch of drinks or are really winning big and feeling a little more generous. If luck is pretty bad, the normal tip will do.

It is also customary at the machines to tip the changeperson, especially if you're winning big. For example, if you win several hundred dollars (or several thousand dollars), you may want to spread a little love around to the changepeople who have helped you. If you really get lucky and win the jackpot, you may want to spread a lot of love around.

If you're losing or not doing anything special at the machines, you really don't need to be giving out gratuities to the changepeople. Tips, the way I look at it, need only be given by winners – you've already donated enough to the coffers. Tips usually won't be expected from losers, unless a changeperson has given you such incredible service that you feel obligated.

By the way, so you know how to talk the talk, tips are known as **tokes** in the casino.

4. THE ELEMENTS OF A VIDEO POKER MACHINE

Video Poker machines are composed of various functioning parts you should be familiar with, and we'll go over them in this chapter.

THE MACHINE
The Payout Display
On the top of each video poker machine will be a **payout display** showing all the combinations of cards that will be winners and the number of coins or absolute dollar amounts that will be paid when you win.

The payout display will show the winning payouts for every coin played. If the machine is a progressive, the display will either show the progressive total on the machine itself or be marked "Progressive." When "Progressive" is indicated on the payout display, that progressive jackpot total will be displayed prominently on a large sign above the bank of progressive machines.

Service Light/Candle Light
On top of each slot machine will be a red indicator light, known as the **Service Light**, or **Candle Light**, which will

light up whenever the services of a slots employee is needed. The red light will be activated (that is, lit) when the player presses the CHANGE button requesting assistance, when the machine malfunctions, or when a jackpot is hit and the machine is unable to payout the full number of coins. The last condition is the one we really like to see – that and all the noise that comes with it, too.

The Coin Tray
On the bottom facing of each machine is a metal tray, called the **coin tray**. This is where the coins pour out of the machine when the CASH OUT button is pushed.

THE PLAY BUTTONS
In this section, I'll describe the active play buttons you might find on a video poker machine. Note that some of the buttons listed may have slightly different names, depending upon the manufacturer. In general, though, whether they're called by one name or another, they serve the same function.

Deal/Draw Button
When you insert coins into the machine or play fewer than the full number of credits, you will have to press the DEAL button to get a hand of five cards dealt to you.

Play Max Credits/Bet Max Coins
Pressing the PLAY MAX CREDITS button will play the full number of credits allowed on the machine and automatically deal the cards. Thus, if the machine accepts five coins as a bet, pressing PLAY MAX CREDITS will deduct five coins from your credits. Similarly, if three coins are

the maximum bet, then three coins will be played and that amount will be deducted.

This button may also be called BET MAX COINS or PLAY ALL CREDITS. It may also have another similar designation such as PLAY FIVE COINS, which would amount to the same thing. The PLAY MAX CREDITS button will activate the game (and deduct the coins played) only if you have credit. If there is no credit accrued in the machine, you will have to insert more money into the heart of the beast and play off that until credits are reestablished.

Play One Credit
For players who prefer to play one credit at a time, video poker machines have a "PLAY ONE CREDIT" button. Pressing this button will play one credit toward the next hand. Note: this will not automatically activate the game as the PLAY MAX CREDITS button will. Nothing will happen – that is, cards will not be dealt – until you press the DEAL button.

You can also play two credits by pressing the "Play One Credit" button twice, or three credits by pressing it three times, or the maximum number of credits by pressing this button until the full allowance of coins is reached.

This button may also read as BET ONE COIN or PLAY ONE CREDIT or have another similar designation amounting to the same thing.

The Cash Out Button
The CASH OUT button, when pressed, converts all the

credits built up over the playing session into coins that drop like a metal waterfall into the coin drop below.

Players use the CASH OUT button, which is located prominently on the front of the machine, when they're ready to change machines, to call it a day at the machines altogether, or simply to hear the victory charge of coins pounding into the coin drop. The sound of coins dropping is always fun!

The Change Button
On the far left position on the button display will be a CHANGE button. This convenient button brings you door-to-door service from the changeperson. As I've noted, pressing the CHANGE button lights up the red candle light at the top of your machine and lets the attendants know that you need service.

THE DISPLAYS
There will be several displays on the front of the machine. While different slots may display the information in different locations and include things others won't, the basic information will remain the same and be part of any modern video poker machine.

Credits Played or Coins Played
The **Credits Played** display shows how many coins are being bet on this particular spin. This display may also be listed as **Coins Played**. Thus, if three coins are played, the display would indicate the number "3" for your information.

ELEMENTS OF A VIDEO POKER MACHINE

Credits

The **Credits** indicator shows how many credits you have accumulated either through winning hands or through money entered into the machine. Each credit shown will reflect the denomination of coin you're playing.

For example, placing a $20 bill into a 25¢ machine will enter eighty 25¢ credits into your account. The indicator in Credits will read "80." If you play three credits, the Credits will read "77," and if that spin is a win for twenty credits, the Credits will read "97" to reflect the twenty coins you won. If you entered that $20 in a dollar machine, then twenty credits "20" would be entered.

Pressing the PLAY ONE CREDIT or PLAY ALL CREDITS button will automatically deduct those credits from your bankroll.

You can use your credits either by playing them through until the total is down to 0 (which means you've lost them all!) or hitting the CASH OUT button, which will convert credit into actual coins and send them noisily tumbling into the coin well.

Winner Paid

The **Winner Paid** indicator displays the amount you won on the current spin. For example, if you make a Full House on a Jacks or Better machine playing the full five coins, you may win forty coins. In this instance, the Winner Paid display will read "40."

Insert Coin

When the machine is awaiting a play, the **Insert Coin** message will be lit. This lets the player know that he or she will need to drop some action into the machine to initiate play.

Error Code

There is another indicator on the front of the machine, by the others, and this is the error code indicator. Should the machine malfunction in some fashion, the error code indicator will display a code number that will alert the technician to the nature of the problem so he can address it and get your machine fixed. You won't typically see this in action since it will light up only when there is a problem.

SECTION B
- VIDEO POKER VARIETIES -

5. INTRODUCTION

The original version of video poker, Jacks or Better, has created a springboard for a host of varieties and offshoots. Games with wild cards have been introduced, such as Deuces Wild and Joker Wild. Single, double, and triple progressive machines have sparked enormous interest among players. Variations with various forms of card replacement, multiple deck action, and differing payout structures from all the above have made video poker a many-headed animal.

Sometimes the new variations of video poker give you a very good chance of being a winner – if not an outright edge – if you follow the correct strategies. On the other hand, many of these games are deceptive in their lures and give the house an edge that is really tough to overcome.

We'll look at all these versions, good and bad, and I'll give you the best strategies to follow regardless of which game you're playing. Due to the enormity of variations, we will not be able to cover every type of machine and payout schedule you may find, but overall, we'll cover the most important games. When you're finished reading, you'll have a good understanding of how to beat video poker machines wherever they may be found.

Despite the many innovative versions of video poker that have been introduced since the original Jacks or Better made its appearance, to this day, Jacks or Better, in its more or less original form, remains the basic version of the game preferred by players. At the same time, all these new variations are either catching on or falling by the wayside and being replaced by yet another set of innovations.

Video poker machines can be categorized into several sections, as I've done here. There are Jacks or Better Varieties (games based on the original concept using a hand of jacks as the minimum payout). There are 10's or Better and Two Pair Varieties (the minimum payout being 10's or the two pair varieties). There are also Wild Card Varieties (games using wild cards), Multiple Deck Varieties (games being dealt with multiple decks), and Specialty Varieties (for machines that don't quite fall into the other categories).

Before we get into the categories of machines as listed above, we'll take a brief look at the difference between Flat-Top and Progressive video poker machines.

PROGRESSIVES & NON-PROGRESSIVES

Video poker offers the player a variety of machines from which to choose. One way of classifying video poker machines is to look at them as **Flat-Top** (or **Straight**) machines and as **Progressives**. There are many forms of video poker machines within these types of categories, and indeed, we will categorize the types of machines we will find differently in this book, but for now, let's look at the difference between the non-progressive and progressive video poker varieties.

Flat-Tops or Straight Machines
The Flat-Tops or Straight machines offer set payoffs on all the hands you win, with the payoffs proportionately larger for greater number of coins played. Thus, a winning payoff on two coins played will be exactly double that for the same winning hand with one coin played.

The one exception is for the royal flush, where a winning payoff on a machine may give you, for example, a 4,000 coin return when five coins are played, as opposed to only 200, 400, 600 and 800 coins on a one, two, three and four coin play respectively. All other payoffs are in proportion.

Winning payoffs are posted on the machine, so you can see right off what you're up against.

Progressive Machines
The Progressive machines differ from the Straight or Flat Tops in that when a royal flush is hit with five coins played, the payoff is not a set amount but is based on a progressive total. This jackpot constantly increases until the royal is hit; then it starts again at a set amount, such as $1,000 on a 25¢ machine.

The Progressives can be exciting – jackpots go higher and higher, and now and again, a quarter machine will soar well into the $2,000+ range or even higher. However, as on the Straight machines, you must play the full five coins to reap the full reward when you hit the royal flush.

Progressives are of two general types. One type is the local progressive network, where a bank of machines in a carousel are hooked up into the same progressive jackpot. There may be six machines or as many as a dozen or more. The typical winning hand on these machines is a royal flush, and while the jackpots are large, they pale in comparison with the wide-area progressive machines.

The other type of progressives are the machines that are hooked up city-wide or even state-wide. On these wide-area network machines, the jackpot hand is much rarer (and almost impossible to hit), but the progressive jackpots can get to enormous amounts.

For example, the hand needed to win the wide area progressive might be a sequential royal flush, where the royal flush must be hit in order, say left to right – 10, J, Q, K, and A. Having the royal show up in the order of J, 10, K, A, Q, would be well and good for winning the standard royal flush payout, and it's certainly nothing to complain about, but on a wide area network requiring a royal flush in a particular order, it wouldn't qualify for the monster jackpot.

The chances of winning sequential types of royals are similar to the chances of winning a lottery – they're astronomical. In other words, don't count your chickens, because it's probably not going to happen to you. The disadvantage to playing wide-area progressives with lottery-type jackpots is that the payoff schedules for the regular hands have been adjusted downwards, and you'll be playing at a large disadvantage while trying for the big hit. I generally recommend against playing these machines – to feed the giant jackpot, more coins have to be taken off the small payoffs, and the overall result is an unprofitable situation for the player.

We'll talk more about progressives later when we discuss each game individually. For now, let's understand the concept of full pay and short pay machines.

FULL PAY VS. SHORT PAY

The payout schedules I'm generally showing in this book are considered **full pay** machines – machines with the best basic payout schedules found for their type. In the full pay category, we basically judge the payout schedule for hands other than a royal flush, since you can find progressives and certain specialty machines that pay extraordinarily well for the royal flush.

For example, if a machine or progressive pays 5,500 coins for a royal flush, as opposed to a more standard 4,000 coins on a Jacks or Better machine, we would still call the 4,000 coin machine a full pay if the other payouts were at a full pay level. However, if the full house paid only six coins and the flush five coins for each coin played, than that machine would be considered a short pay since it is less than the standard nine coins and six coins, respectively, of a full pay Jacks or Better.

The full pay machines are generally found in competitive

locations in competitive markets, most notably the Las Vegas market. The full pay machines are the best to play since they give the best return, often close to 100%, sometimes even more. But in all cases, as the full pay concept suggests, you will get the best payouts available, and thus the best game and the best chances of winning.

The other type of payout schedules, the **short pay** ones, pay less than the optimal amount found on the full pays. As a whole, they are machines you want to avoid. The rate of loss is much greater on those than on full pays, since the payoffs are poorer. You will be playing at a larger disadvantage than you would like. The smaller payout of returns on winning hands adds up quickly in video poker since the rate of play is so fast, and you'll see that difference quickly in your shrunken bankroll.

You'll feel those lesser payouts fast, particularly when they affect hands on the lower end of the pay schedule – hands such as two pairs, for example, which will show up frequently.

There are many different payout schedules for short pay Jacks or Better machines, and if you are familiar with the full pay machines that I've shown, you will readily see where you get shorted. On exceptionally lousy short pay machines, which you'll find where competition for your video poker dollar is non-existent or virtually non-existent (cruise lines are an example – where players are a captive audience), returns will be shorted almost across the board, and you will get pounded mightily by the terrible payouts.

In locations where competition might be a little more fierce, just one payout may be altered, making the machine appear to be a full pay. But on closer inspection, you may see that all looks good except that you get only one coin for a two pair, as opposed to the full pay two coins.

Short pay machines are more likely to be found where players will play video poker for the sake of playing and are less concerned with getting the best payback schedule possible. For example, in Las Vegas, machines located in convenience stores (which are typically allowed up to seven machines) and airports are like those on the cruise ships mentioned above – players are more of a captive audience, and will play despite the poorer odds of the short pays. In the busy strip and downtown casinos, competition is more fierce, and full pays are needed to maximize play and casino returns. People will tend to avoid poorer paying machines.

A favorite trick of these short pay machines is either to pay just one coin on a two pair hand, with the rest of the payout schedule being standard, or six and five coins respectively on the full house and flush – as opposed to the full pay nine and six payouts. To the casual player, these short pays don't seem too costly. In fact, though, they bring down the return percentage significantly. Serious players avoid short pay machines becasue the odds are stacked up against them – you should, too.

Let's now look at the basic video poker games you may find, starting with Jacks or Better.

6. JACKS OR BETTER VARIETIES

Despite the many innovative versions of video poker that have been introduced since the original Jacks or Better made its appearance, still to this day, Jacks or Better, in its more or less original form, remains the basic version of the game preferred by players and found virtually everywhere video poker is played.

In this section, we'll look at the standard Jacks or Better games and the progressive, bonus quad, and bonus royal varieties.

JACKS OR BETTER 9-6 MACHINES

Following is a common paytable for the basic version of Jacks or Better. This paytable is sometimes referred to as the "9-6" machine, so-named for the payoff on the full house and flush respectively. This is opposed to the "8-5" machine, the common payout found on the progressives.

PAYTABLE ON JACKS OR BETTER
Full Pay 9-6 Machine

Coins Played	1	2	3	4	5
Royal Flush	250	500	750	1000	4000
Straight Flush	50	100	150	200	250
Four-of-a-kind	25	50	75	100	125
Full House	9	18	27	36	45
Flush	6	12	18	24	30
Straight	4	8	12	16	20
Three-of-a-kind	3	6	9	12	15
Two Pair	2	4	6	8	10
Jacks or Better	1	2	3	4	5

The minimum hand needed to win in this game is a pair of jacks; any lesser pair or hand pays nothing. The greater the strength of the hand, of course, the larger the payout. Lesser payoffs will be found for similar winning combinations, and we'll discuss them in the strategy section. For now, though, know that this is the basic paytable found in competitive markets like Las Vegas.

The 9-6 machines with the payoffs shown below give you a payback of about 99.5% – that's a pretty good game if you follow my strategies. Machines that pay only five coins for the flush cost you about 1%. When only six coins are paid for a full house and five coins for a flush, the overall payback is about 95%. It costs you about 4-1/2% from the full payback schedule.

JACKS OR BETTER VARIETIES

JACKS OR BETTER 8-5 MACHINES (SHORT PAY)

This Jacks or Better short pay machine is identical to the one above, except that the payouts on the full house and flush respectively, are eight and five, as opposed to the nine and six of the 9-6 machines. The cost of the lower paybacks on these hands is a little over 2% – they give you an overall payback of 97.3%. That's not the ideal full payback you want, and it's not a payback schedule I recommend.

On the 8-5 progressives below, which do have an identical payback schedule, the loss of the few percent for these hands is made up by a larger progressive payout on the royal flush – provided, of course, that the progressive is high enough.

JACKS OR BETTER 8-5 PROGRESSIVES

The progressive Jacks or Better machines are really exciting. They give players a chance to win big dollars should they get lucky enough to hit the royal flush when the progressive has accumulated a large total. As you'll see in the strategy section, the best way to play the progressives is to play only when the progressives have grown large enough to tilt the odds.

At reset, right after a royal flush has been hit and the jackpot is set back to the starting point, the payback schedule is one-half percent higher than a non-progressive 8-5 machine. This is due to the progressive starting point of 5,250 coins.

Keep in mind, though, that progressive payouts are not expressed in terms of coin amounts, but in dollars. A 25¢ machine will typically start out with a $1,250 jackpot for the royal, and $4,000 for $1 machines. As the progressive grows larger (it will typically be at the 5,250 coin level immediately after a royal has been hit), so does the payback percentage for the player.

A full 100% payback will be reached on this progressive when the jackpot reaches $2,200 on a 25¢ machine, or $8,800 on a $1 machine. (The break-even is actually closer to $2,170, but I'm rounding up). A 6-5 progressive is worse for the player. It drops the starting payback to under 96% and makes the break-even point of the jackpot a full $1,000 higher – about $3,300.

PAYTABLE ON JACKS OR BETTER
8-5 Progressives

Coins Played	1	2	3	4	5
Royal Flush	250	500	750	1000	Prog.
Straight Flush	50	100	150	200	250
Four-of-a-kind	25	50	75	100	125
Full House	8	16	24	32	40
Flush	5	10	15	20	25
Straight	4	8	12	16	20
Three-of-a-kind	3	6	9	12	15
Two Pair	2	4	6	8	10
Jacks or Better	1	2	3	4	5

BONUS QUADS

These Jacks or Better variations, which come in a number of flavors, offer extra bonus payouts for specified four of a kind hands, called **quads**. For example, the machine may give a higher payout if you get four aces or four deuces. There are many types of quads available, but they all work according to the same principle – you receive an extra bonus if you hit the quad or quads specified. The special quad bonus available will be posted on the machine itself.

Lower down on the paytable, hands such as two pair are adjusted downward – you get smaller paybacks for those as a counterweight for the extra bonuses paid on the quad winners. However, the high extra returns paid for the quads often compensate and make these among the best-percentage video poker machines in the Nevada market. As a result, the bonus quads are a popular variations. At the Gulf Coast casinos in Mississippi and Louisiana, and at other locations where paytables are typically much less favorable, you will more than likely find short pay machines with less attractive payouts that are not very favorable to the player.

The bonus quads, which are typically found as non-progressive machines, have many variations all working from the same premise – extra payouts on four-of-a-kind hands. In the very popular IGT varieties, you'll see Double Bonus Poker (97.8% payback), Bonus Poker Deluxe (98.5% payback), Double Double Bonus (99% payback), and other varieties by various manufacturers such as Aces and Eights, Super Aces, and more.

Note that the payback percentages have everything to do with the payout schedules, which you will see in a myriad of possibilities, depending upon where you play and the current thinking of the host location. For example, you might find a Double Double Bonus game that offers ten coins per coin played on a full house and seven coins on a flush (as opposed to the nine and six I show here), and that would make the payback schedule at just over 100% with optimal play.

Take a look at some of the payoffs for these bonus quads:

PAYTABLE ON JACKS OR BETTER
Double Bonus Poker

Coins Played	1	2	3	4	5
Royal Flush	250	500	750	1000	4000
Straight Flush	50	100	150	200	250
Four Aces	160	320	480	640	800
Four 2-4s	80	160	240	320	400
Four 5-Ks	50	100	150	200	250
Full House	9	18	27	36	45
Flush	6	12	18	24	30
Straight	5	10	15	20	25
Three-of-a-kind	3	6	9	12	15
Two Pairs	1	2	3	4	5
Jacks or Better	1	2	3	4	5

PAYTABLE ON JACKS OR BETTER
Bonus Poker Deluxe

Coins Played	1	2	3	4	5
Royal Flush	250	500	750	1000	4000
Straight Flush	50	100	150	200	250
Four-of-a-kind	80	160	240	320	400
Full House	8	16	24	32	40
Flush	6	12	18	24	30
Straight	4	8	12	16	20
Three-of-a-kind	3	6	9	12	15
Two Pairs	1	2	3	4	5
Jacks or Better	1	2	3	4	5

PAYTABLE ON JACKS OR BETTER
Double Double Bonus

Coins Played	1	2	3	4	5
Royal Flush	250	500	750	1000	4000
Straight Flush	50	100	150	200	250
Four As and 2-4[a]	400	800	1200	1600	2000
Four 2-4 and A-4[b]	160	320	480	640	800
Four Aces	160	320	480	640	800
Four 2-4s	80	160	240	320	400
Four 5-Ks	50	100	150	200	250
Full House	9	18	27	36	45
Flush	6	12	18	24	30
Straight	4	8	12	16	20
Three-of-a-kind	3	6	9	12	15
Two Pairs	1	2	3	4	5
Jacks or Better	1	2	3	4	5

a - A hand of four Aces with the fifth card being a 2, 3, or 4

b - A hand of four 2s, four 3s, or four 4s, with the fifth card being an Ace, 2, 3, or 4.

BONUS ROYALS

The bonus royal machines come in two varieties, as non-progressives and progressives. On the bonus royal machines, the player gets a bonus payout for hitting a specified type of royal flush. For example, the machine might specify a royal flush in hearts for the big bonus, or might specify that the royal flush has to be consecutive left to right, with the 10 being the first card on the left, the jack, the next card, and so on to the king, which would be the last card to the right.

On the non-progressive machines, the bonus payout will be tied to a specific payout enumerated on the paytable of the machine. The progressives, however, will tie that winning hand into the progressive total, and if it is hit, the lucky player will win the current amount shown on the progressive.

Getting a regular royal on these machines is like getting one on any other machine. Scoring the bonus royal with the extra restrictions is really rare. It is very hard to hit a royal flush of any type, let alone one with qualifications that make it so much more rare.

The following machine shows a payback of close to 100% for the player, weighing in at a very attractive 99.7% with proper play. Other payback schedules can increase that payback or reduce it, depending on the payoffs given for the various winners.

PAYTABLE ON JACKS OR BETTER
Bonus Royal

Coins Played	1	2	3	4	5
Royal Flush (sp)	500	1000	1500	2000	10000
Royal Flush	250	500	750	1000	5000
Straight Flush (sp)	100	200	300	400	500
Straight Flush	50	100	150	200	250
Four-of-a-kind	25	50	75	100	125
Full House	8	16	24	32	40
Flush (sp)	10	20	30	40	50
Flush	5	10	15	20	25
Straight	4	8	12	16	20
Three-of-a-kind	3	6	9	12	15
Two Pairs	2	4	6	8	10
Jacks or Better	1	2	3	4	5

sp - Specified. For example, if the machine calls for a royal flush or straight flush in hearts, that hand must be hit to achieve the stated payout.

7. TENS OR BETTER VARIETIES

The Tens or Better machines, which are more rare now, are the same as Jacks or Better except that the minimum winning hand for a payout is a pair of 10s. While there are more frequent payouts with a Tens or Better machine, the payout schedule has been adjusted downward to compensate. Some Tens or Better machines have good payouts, but the majority of them do not, which accounts for the fading popularity of this variation.

The 6-5 Tens or Better variation shown here has a payback of 99.1% with proper play. That's not too bad; it's certainly playable. However, beware of Tens or Better machines that pay more on the full houses and flushes but reduce the two pair payout to just one coin per coin played as opposed to two. That can reduce the payout by as much as 10% or more.

SECRETS OF WINNING VIDEO POKER

PAYTABLE ON TENS OR BETTER
Full Pay 6-5 Machine

Coins Played	1	2	3	4	5
Royal Flush	250	500	750	1000	4000
Straight Flush	50	100	150	200	250
Four-of-a-kind	25	50	75	100	125
Full House	6	12	18	24	30
Flush	5	10	15	20	25
Straight	4	8	12	16	20
Three-of-a-kind	3	6	9	12	15
Two Pair	2	4	6	8	10
10s or Better	1	2	3	4	5

TWO PAIRS OR BETTER

Again, this is not a common machine, and you shouldn't confuse it with the Joker Wild: Two Pair game. You can find from time to time. The minimum winning hand is two pair. A pair of tens or jacks doesn't cut the mustard in this game, nor do aces. You need at least two pair or better to qualify for a return.

Not being able to win on any single pair greatly reduces the frequency of winning; this is compensated for with higher payouts on the hands you can win. Some of the payouts will get you close to a 98% return with proper strategy, which is not bad. But many machines featuring poorer payout schedules drop you many points below that level. They're not good machines to play if you're trying to win.

The following paytables show you a full pay and a short

pay. The first one – the 8-6 variety – is the much more favorable one, at about a 98% payback. The second machine reduces the overall payback to only 93.5% – avoid it like the plague.

PAYTABLE ON TWO PAIR OR BETTER
No Wild Cards - Full Pay

Coins Played	1	2	3	4	5
Royal Flush	250	500	750	1000	4000
Straight Flush	100	200	300	400	500
Four-of-a-kind	50	100	150	200	250
Full House	12	24	36	48	60
Flush	8	16	24	32	40
Straight	6	12	18	24	30
Three-of-a-kind	3	6	9	12	15
Two Pairs	2	4	6	8	10

PAYTABLE ON TWO PAIR OR BETTER
No Wild Cards - Short Pay

Coins Played	1	2	3	4	5
Royal Flush	250	500	750	1000	4000
Straight Flush	100	200	300	400	500
Four-of-a-kind	50	100	150	200	250
Full House	11	22	33	44	55
Flush	7	14	21	28	35
Straight	5	10	15	20	25
Three-of-a-kind	3	6	9	12	15
Two Pairs	2	4	6	8	10

8. WILD CARD VARIETIES

JOKER WILD - ACE-KING

There are two versions of the Joker Wild game: Ace-King and Two Pairs. In the Ace-King version, a minimum hand of a pair of kings must be made for a payoff. In Two Pairs, two pair is the minimum hand needed for a payoff. Both versions of Joker Wild are played with a 53-card deck – the regular 52-card deck plus the wild card, the joker, which can be assigned any value.

We'll look at the payoffs for each Joker Wild game. Note that the royal flush will be paid off with the maximum return only if five coins are played. You'll notice also that the high pair hands – aces and kings – get the same payoff as a two pair hand. The payoff schedule shown here is very favorable for the player, providing a return of 100.6% with perfect play.

Sometimes a machine will be found that pays off only 15 for 1 on the four-of-a-kind instead of the 20 for 1 as listed above. Give these poorer paying machines a miss if you can, and stick to the better payouts of the varieties paying 20 for 1.

AYTABLE ON JOKER WILD
Ace-King

Coins Played	1	2	3	4	5
Royal Flush (nat)	250	500	750	1000	4000
Five-of-a-kind	200	400	600	800	1000
Royal Flush (jok)	100	200	300	400	500
Straight Flush	50	100	150	200	250
Four-of-a-kind	20	40	60	80	100
Full House	7	14	21	28	35
Flush	5	10	15	20	25
Straight	3	6	9	12	15
Three-of-a-kind	2	4	6	8	10
Two Pair	1	2	3	4	5
Ace or Kings	1	2	3	4	5

nat - Natural. No wild cards.

jok - Indicates that the royal flush is made using the joker.

JOKER WILD - TWO PAIR

Now let's look at the payout schedule for the other type of joker wild machine, the two pair game. Note that five coins must be played – and should always be played – to receive the maximum payout for the royal flush. For example, the royal flush will pay out 4,000 coins or $1,000 for a quarter machine when five coins are played, while four coins would yield only 1/4 as much – $250.

Getting a straight flush with five coins will pay 250 coins (or $62.50) and a full house will pay forty-five coins (or $11.25) for that same quarter machine. The payout schedule below gives a 98.7% return with proper play. There are

25¢ machine, $4,000 on a $1 machine). That's not too bad as a starting point, particularly since you will usually catch the progressive as it is already growing. At the $1,600 level on a 25¢ machine, or $6,400 on a $1 one, you'll reach 100%; anything over that, and you're playing with the percentages in your favor.

PAYOFFS ON DEUCES WILD PROGRESSIVE
Full Pay

Coins Played	1	2	3	4	5
Royal Flush (nat)	250	500	750	1000	Prog.
Four Deuces	200	400	600	800	1000
Royal Flush (wild)	25	50	75	100	125
Five-of-a-kind	15	30	45	60	75
Straight Flush	9	18	27	36	45
Four-of-a-kind	4	8	12	16	20
Full House	4	8	12	16	20
Flush	3	6	9	12	15
Straight	2	4	6	8	10
Three-of-a-kind	1	2	3	4	5

nat - Natural. No wild cards.
wild - Indicates that the royal flush is made using a wild 2.

DEUCES AND JOKER WILD

Five wild cards in a 53-card deck results in a very lively game. Over half the hands are potential winners, although they are mostly pushes. The minimum winning hand is three-of-a-kind; note that there is also a payout for holding five wild cards. A hand with the joker and the four deuces is more difficult to get than a natural royal flush, and, as you'll see on the paytable, it pays out the most – 10,000 coins if five coins were played.

Deuces and Joker Wild machines have an excellent 99% payback in some Nevada casinos (paytable A – Full Pay), though there are versions found along the Mississippi that pay only 93% (paytable B – Short Pay). The second paytable has really poor payoffs compared to the first one. You should avoid machines like this; they'll eat you alive fast.

PAYTABLE ON DEUCES AND JOKER WILD
Paytable A - Full Pay

Coins Played	1	2	3	4	5
Five Wild Cards	1000	2000	3000	4000	10000
Royal Flush (nat)	250	500	750	1000	4000
Four Deuces	25	50	75	100	125
Royal Flush (wild)	12	24	36	48	60
Five-of-a-kind	9	18	27	36	45
Straight Flush	6	12	18	24	30
Four-of-a-kind	3	6	9	12	15
Full House	3	6	9	12	15
Flush	3	6	9	12	15
Straight	3	6	9	12	15
Three-of-a-kind	1	2	3	4	5

nat - Natural. No wild cards.
wild - Indicates that the royal flush is made using a wild 2.

PAYTABLE ON DEUCES AND JOKER WILD
Paytable B - Short Pay

Coins Played	1	2	3	4	5
Five Wild Cards	250	500	750	1000	2500
Royal Flush (nat)	400	800	1200	1600	2000
Four Deuces	100	200	300	400	500
Royal Flush (wild)	20	40	60	80	100
Five-of-a-kind	12	24	36	48	60
Straight Flush	7	14	21	28	35
Four-of-a-kind	3	6	9	12	15
Full House	2	4	6	8	10
Flush	2	4	6	8	10
Straight	1	2	3	4	5
Three-of-a-kind	1	2	3	4	5

nat - Natural. No wild cards.

wild - Indicates that the royal flush is made using a wild 2.

9. MULTIPLE DECK VARIETIES

In this section we'll look at video poker games using multiple decks of cards – Triple Play, Five Deck Poker, and Five Deck Frenzy. (Note that the strategies for the five deck games in this section are beyond the scope of this book, but we'll take a brief look at how they are played anyway.)

TRIPLE PLAY

This interesting variation features the simultaneous play of three hands, hence the name "triple play." Three hands of five cards each are displayed face down on the screen – only the backs of the cards are shown. When coins are inserted or credits are played and the Deal/Draw button is pressed, all five cards of the bottom hand are exposed. The cards in the other two hands – the middle and top hands – remain face down.

You select the best cards to hold in the exposed hand by pressing the hold button, and, as with standard machines everywhere, you can toggle back and forth, selecting and deselecting the cards to be held by pressing the hold button under the corresponding cards. When you've made your final decision, press the Deal/Draw button on the machine to discard the unwanted cards and receive new ones on the draw.

The cards that are held in the bottom hand will be held in the other two hands as well. Thus, if you choose a jack of hearts and queen of spades to hold, all three hands will display the jack of hearts and queen of spades in the same relative positions. The three unchosen cards in the top two hands will remain face down. In essence, you have three separate hands holding a jack of hearts and queen of spades.

When you press the Deal/Draw button, the three unwanted cards on the original hand shown at the bottom get discarded, and three new cards get turned over one at a time, from left to right. The same process happens on the second hand, the one above the bottom one, and then finally on the third and top one, one card at a time, from left to right.

Each of the three hands will be dealt separately from its own deck so that three unique hands are formed. (Cards that were held before the draw are removed from the deck.) Each hand will display the held cards – the jack and the queen in this example – plus the three new drawn cards. The hands will be paid separately according to the number of coins bet and the winning combinations as displayed on the machine.

Let's look at one more example to make this perfectly clear. Let's say that you're dealt J J 7 8 K, and you hold the jacks. Thus, the pair of jacks will show up on all three hands as the held cards. It's a good start so far, with three automatic winners. On the first hand, you may get dealt J 2 4 for a three-of-a-kind, on the second 6 6 8 for two pair, and the third A K 2 for a pair of jacks. You would have three winners in this example, with payouts for trips, two pair, and jacks.

On the other hand, you could get dealt the original hand of 2 5 6 9 J, hold the jack, get dealt garbage cards, and end up with no paying combinations on any of the three hands for a total loss.

On the Triple Play machine, all three hands are activated only if at least three coins are wagered. Betting one coin activates just one hand, betting two activates the second hand, and betting three activates all three hands of the machine. To the right and left of each hand, a small number appears showing how many coins are bet on that hand.

You can continue betting up to fifteen coins total, five coins per hand. For example, if you played only four coins total, the bottom hand would display a "2" showing that two coins are bet, and the other two hands would display a "1," for a grand total of four coins bet. An additional coin bet would go toward the middle hand, which would also display a "2." A sixth coin inserted would give the top hand a 2-coin play as well. Each coin inserted will be added to hands in this fashion, from bottom to top, until a maximum of five hands per hand are bet.

Hands are paid separately according to the number of coins wagered in their position.

SECRETS OF WINNING VIDEO POKER

The advantage of playing the full fifteen coins – five coins per position – is that you receive the maximum payout if you hit a royal flush, just as you do in the standard Jacks or Better games. In essence, you're playing for triple the stakes at Triple Play by wagering on three machines simultaneously.

The illustrations on the following pages show how the triple play machines work.

MULTIPLE DECK VARIETIES

TRIPLE PLAY - HOW IT WORKS

Illustration A - The player's original five-card hand

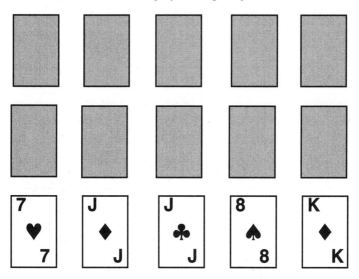

Illustration B - The player holds a pair of jacks

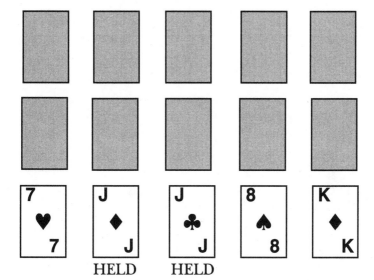

SECRETS OF WINNING VIDEO POKER

TRIPLE PLAY - HOW IT WORKS

Illustration C - The player presses Deal/Draw; three hands of jacks are held

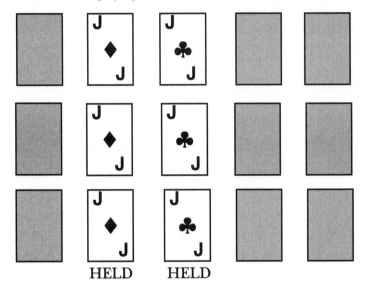

Illustration D - After the Draw, three separate hands are held

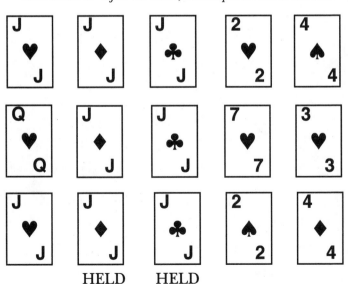

MULTIPLE DECK VARIETIES

FIVE DECK POKER

This interesting twist on the video poker concept uses five separate 52-card decks, with each card position getting cards from its own deck. Thus, let's say you kept an ace of spades in position one and drew four more cards. Since the deck for the second card is unique, you could theoretically draw another ace of spades, and similarly a third one for the next card position. Thus, it is possible to have a hand containing five aces of spades, which would pay 10,000 coins on the non-progressive version if the full five coins were bet.

This same hand, the five aces of spades, would be a huge jackpot winner on a progressive machine. With odds of around 15 million to one against hitting five aces of spades, if you should get so lucky, you would in all likelihood come home with an enormous prize.

The paytable on the following page returns just over 97% to the player. Lesser payouts, of course, will be a poorer proposition for the player.

PAYTABLE ON FIVE DECK POKER
Same Suit Bonuses

Coins Played	1	2	3	4	5
Five-of-a-kind*	1000	2000	3000	4000	10000
Royal Flush	250	500	750	1000	4000
Straight Flush	50	100	150	200	250
Five-of-a-kind	50	100	150	200	250
Four-of-a-kind*	20	40	60	80	100
Full House*	12	24	36	48	60
Four-of-a-kind	10	20	30	40	50
Full House	6	12	18	24	30
Three-of-a-kind*	4	8	12	16	20
Flush	4	8	12	16	20
Straight	3	6	9	12	15
Three-of-a-kind	2	4	6	8	10
Two Pairs*	2	4	6	8	10
Two Pairs	1	2	3	4	5

*Same suit.

FIVE DECK FRENZY

The progressive version of Five Deck Frenzy offers the same 97.1% payback as the non-progressive game before the jackpot starts accumulating. As the progressive increases, so does the payback.

PAYTABLE ON FIVE DECK FRENZY Progressive					
Coins Played	**1**	**2**	**3**	**4**	**5**
Five-of-a-kind*	1000	2000	3000	4000	Prog.
Royal Flush	250	500	750	1000	4000
Straight Flush	50	100	150	200	250
Five-of-a-kind	50	100	150	200	250
Four-of-a-kind*	20	40	60	80	100
Full House*	12	24	36	48	60
Four-of-a-kind	10	20	30	40	50
Full House	6	12	18	24	30
Three-of-a-kind*	4	8	12	16	20
Flush	4	8	12	16	20
Straight	3	6	9	12	15
Three-of-a-kind	2	4	6	8	10
Two Pairs*	2	4	6	8	10
Two Pairs	1	2	3	4	5

*Same suit.

10. SPECIALTY VARIETIES

DOUBLE DOWN STUD

This variation deals you four cards and then gives you the option to double your bet before receiving the fifth card. There are no draws as in the other variations and no choices on which cards to keep and which ones to get rid of. You get only five cards total.

Here, your only task is to evaluate whether the first four cards have enough strength to warrant doubling of your bet. Once you've made the decision to double (or not), the fifth card is revealed by the machine and the full five-card hand will be exposed.

The game is played for up to five coins initially, but if you hit the double button, that bet will be doubled. Thus, if you had initially wagered five coins, hitting the doubling button will increase that bet to ten coins. At the same time, all the payoffs will be doubled as well. The payoff chart will scroll on the machine so that you can see the paytable for the larger bet size.

What happens if you have only five coins in the machine and hit the double button? No problem. Simply insert five more coins (or bills) into the machine. The amount needed will be deducted automatically for the bet and the leftover money, if there is any, will be added to your credits.

The strategy decisions are fairly simple, and we'll cover them later in the strategy section. At this juncture, I will let you know that I do not recommend the double down variation.

Following is a Double Down Stud Progressive pay chart such as you might find in Las Vegas.

PAYTABLE ON DOUBLE DOWN STUD
Progressive

Coins Played	1	2	3	4	5
Royal Flush	1000	2000	3000	4000	Prog.
Straight Flush	200	400	600	800	1000
Four-of-a-kind	50	100	150	200	250
Full House	12	24	36	48	60
Flush	9	18	27	36	45
Straight	6	12	18	24	30
Three-of-a-kind	4	8	12	16	20
Two Pair	3	6	9	12	15
Jacks-Aces	2	4	6	8	10
6s-10s	1	2	3	4	5

DOUBLE OR NOTHING OPTION

Some video poker machines now feature a double up option, an even money betting proposition that allows you to double your take on winning hands. Here's how it works: whenever a winning hand is concluded, the machine gives you the option of pressing the doubling button. If you ignore this button, you'll win the standard payout shown. If you press the double button, five cards will be dealt.

One card will be an upcard, and that is the dealer's hand. For you to win, you must choose one of the four face down cards (by clicking on it) and have that card be of higher value than the dealer's upcard. If it's higher, you win; if it's lower you lose. For this purpose ace is high and deuce is low. In the case of equal value – say you both have a 7 – then it is a push (a tie), and the double bet will be replayed.

The doubling feature gives the house no edge at all. It's an even money proposition – an old fashioned double or nothing bet. You can keep doubling this bet until you lose it all, or you can cash out.

DOUBLE CARD JACKS OR BETTER

This *seemingly* attractive game, which is a Jacks or Better variation, uses a 53-card deck. This 53rd card is actually an extra card – a double of one of the other cards in the deck. When you get this card in your hand, your payout is doubled. This 53rd card is not to be confused with a wild card – it isn't one. It serves only to double existing winners, and when you hold it, it effectively reduces the hand to a four-card hand.

We'll discuss this more in the strategy section. For now, suffice it to say that the doubled card is not advantageous to the player and this is not a game I recommend.

SECRETS OF WINNING VIDEO POKER

PICK FIVE

The Pick Five machines present an interesting twist on the standard Jacks or Better theme. Rather than getting five cards dealt right off the bat, you receive just two in the upper right part of the screen. You choose one of these cards and that becomes the first card in your hand; that card will be displayed in the lower part of the screen, with the other four card spaces blank or showing just the backs. The card you don't choose will be discarded. Note that discarded cards in this game go out of play; they will not appear again in the same deal.

Two more cards will be displayed in the upper right hand screen, and again, you choose one of these cards. This card will be displayed on the bottom of the screen next to the first card chosen, while the card not chosen is discarded and out of play.

Now you have two cards in play. Two fresh cards will again appear on the upper right, and the choosing and discarding process will be repeated here and two more times after, until you have five cards total on the bottom of the screen. That will be your final hand. As in the other video poker games, the payoffs will be based on this five-card hand.

It is much harder to achieve winning hands in Pick Five than in the regular Jacks or Better games, as you will soon see while playing. We'll talk more about this in the strategy section. Meanwhile, take a look at the paytable for this game on the next page.

PAYTABLE ON PICK FIVE POKER
Jacks or Better Basis

Coins Played	1	2	3	4	5
Royal Flush	500	1000	1500	2000	2500
Straight Flush	100	200	300	400	500
Four Aces	320	640	960	1280	1600
Four 2-4s	160	320	480	640	800
Four 5-Ks	80	160	240	320	400
Full House	18	36	54	72	90
Flush	12	24	36	48	60
Straight	8	16	24	32	40
Three-of-a-kind	6	12	18	24	30
Two Pairs	2	4	6	8	10
Jacks or Better	2	4	6	8	10

SECOND CHANCE

The second chance machines allow you to receive a sixth card in an additional "second draw" if the drawing of that one card would give you a chance to make a straight or better hand. Thus, if, after the draw, you have a four-card straight or flush, four-card straight flush or royal flush, two pair, or three- or four- of a kind, a sixth card will appear on the screen and the second chance button will light up. You activate this option by pressing the second chance button and placing an additional one to five coins in the machine.

The good feature of this machine is that you can place any-where from one to five coins as the second chance, even if you bet only one coin originally. The sixth card will be dealt and the machine will automatically choose the five best of the six cards you now hold.

Second chance machines come as both non-progressives and progressives, the latter of which are very good machines for players. We'll talk more about this in the strategy section.

Let's now turn our attention to the winning strategies.

SECTION C
- WINNING STRATEGIES -

11. INTRODUCTION

To win at video poker, you must play the correct strategies. As in regular poker, there are skillful ways to play your hand. Unlike in poker, however, in video poker you're not playing against other players. You're playing against a machine. Strategies that make sense in your Friday night poker game won't make sense in video poker.

The focus of correct play in video poker is on getting winning combinations as listed on the machine. Typically, it requires a hand of at least a pair of jacks to get a payoff. Depending on the variation, though, a pair as low as 6s may achieve a payoff. Or the variation you're playing may require at least a three-of-a-kind for a winner. In all variations, the stronger the hand, the greater the payoff.

In almost all variations, you get the big payoff for the royal flush, as long as you've played five coins. Often 4,000 coins of the denomination played will be the jackpot amount, though on progressive machines, if you play five coins, the total could be a great deal higher, making the game even more interesting.

Due to the enormous payoffs when it is hit, a great deal

of strategy in video poker revolves around the quest to hit the royal flush. In all the strategy tables, you'll see an emphasis on holding cards that will make the royal flush more likely.

Of course, the royal doesn't come often. With correct strategy, you'll hit one every 30,000-40,000 hands on the average, depending, of course, on the variation and strategy you're playing. This doesn't mean, however, that you won't hit one in your very first hour of play. It also doesn't mean that you will hit the royal flush on the 30,000th hand. It can come at any time, often when you least expect it. There are players who have hit two royal flushes in one night, and it has even happened that players got lucky and hit more than two!

Meanwhile, even though you're pursuing the royal flush, you'll also be collecting other winners such as straights, full houses and pairs. With proper play, all in all, you can beat the video poker machines.

The strategies I'll present in this section are designed for easy use under actual casino conditions. My interest here is getting you to play very close to perfectly without having to memorize the many obscure plays that will complicate your decisions and slow you down. The thinking here is the same as in the playing of an advanced card-counting system in blackjack. You sacrifice insignificant small percentages with the goals of faster and easier play, not making mistakes, and playing a more fun and less laborious game.

WINNING STRATEGIES: INTRODUCTION

For example, I have avoided adding memory intensive plays such as two to a royal flush if one of the cards is a 10, or Q J 9 all being suited, or plays requiring you to know how many gaps and high cards are in a particular hand. Including all these in the strategy adds very little to your overall percentage, but it adds complications and increases the chances of error. You want to play a tough game without killing yourself with unnecessary memorization.

So, as a result, I've combined certain complicated plays into one easy-to-use play, which, under certain circumstances, will cause you to make plays that otherwise might not be optimal. However, with a cost typically less than a few tenths of one percent – an amount that will be negligible on your winnings – the minor sacrifice is justified not just for casual players but for pros as well.

Let's now look at the five general strategies of beating the video poker machines. Then we'll turn our attention to the individual strategies needed to beat each variation.

FIVE GENERAL WINNING STRATEGIES
General Strategy #1: Always Play Five Coins
To achieve the absolute best odds at the video poker machine, you must play five coins. At first glance, this suggestion probably strikes you as being strange. Why not one coin or two? After all, the payoffs on all hands at the video poker machine are proportionately the same whether one, two, three, four or five coins are played.

There's one glaring exception to that rule: the royal flush. And though you won't get the royal flush often, you could hit it. Somebody does. Keep in mind that this is not a regular poker game where you may never see a royal flush. It is video poker where you play an entirely different strategy than in the regular table game. Your strategy is focused on the big score – the royal flush.

In a regular poker game, your primary goal is simply to win the hand, even if a pair of 5s do the trick. There is no extra payoff for winning with a royal flush. You win the money in the pot whether your hand is a pair of 5s or a royal. In video poker, there is a difference: 5s don't pay anything, but a royal flush has a huge payout.

You'll play hands in video poker that you wouldn't in a regular poker game and vice-versa. The strategies for the two games are entirely different.

Look at a payoff chart for Jacks or Better and notice what happens on the royal flush payoffs. Interesting, yes? One coin played returns 200 coins, two coins yields 400, three coins 600 and four coins brings home 800 bad boys. Well, the progression for the fifth coin should be 1,000 if you're following along with the addition.

But it's not. The full payoff on a royal flush with five coins played is 4,000 coins!

That's a nice payoff, and it is the reason you're going to play five coins. The royal is not as remote as it seems. As we talked about earlier, you may never see a royal flush in a regular poker game, but at the video poker machines, if you follow the strategies I suggest, you have a chance to land that big fish.

You'll see similar jumps for the royal flush payoffs on most of the video poker machines. Therefore, to collect the full payoff on a royal flush, proper play dictates that you always play the full five coins for each game. If you do hit the royal flush, there's a big, big difference between 1,000 coins returned and 4,000 returned. And on a progressive, the cost of not playing a full five coins will be the progressive itself, which you generally cannot hit unless you play all five coins.

General Strategy #2: Find Machines with the Best Payoffs
The payoff schedules I've listed in this book are the ones commonly found in Las Vegas. Competition among casinos to attract video poker players is keen there, and the payoff schedules, relatively speaking, are good for the player.

The paytables shown here are not the only ones you'll find for the games we've discussed. There are many others offered in casinos around the world. In less competitive places, such as on the Gulf Coast in Mississippi, further up that river, and in Louisiana bars, for example, the pay schedules will often be much less favorable than the ones I've shown here.

You may find machines with less generous payouts in Las Vegas itself as well – even in the same casino. For example, I once noticed that Jacks or Better machines of identical type, just one aisle over from each other in the Mirage Casino on the Las Vegas strip, offered different payout schedules!

So, as a general rule, and when possible, shop around a little to find the best payout schedule – not just within a casino (where like machines will usually have like payouts) – but also among neighboring casinos competing for your attention and business. Keep in mind that when there's a lot of casino competition, such as in Las Vegas, a little window shopping will definitely be to your advantage.

For the same type of machines, depending upon the payout schedule, the payback of machines can vary from 90% on up to over 100% payback, which, of course, is advantageous to the player. I'll identify the relative merits of each machine so you have a good idea of which machines will be more favorable for you to play.

General Strategy #3:
Play Machines that Give You the Best Odds
As we have discussed, there are many types of video poker machines. Some give players a slight edge, some give the casinos a slight edge, and others give the casino a larger edge.

To beat the machines, you must play only the best machines – ones that actually give you the edge if you play properly. At the very least, if you really love other variations, stick to ones that give you a good chance of winning – those in the second category. But what you must do is avoid the machines in that last category, the ones that give the casino a large edge.

With the fast pace of video poker and the great number of coins or credits constantly being played, you need to stick to the better percentage machines to give yourself the best shot at catching a good roll and walking away with profits.

General Strategy #4: Play the Proper Strategies

To give yourself the best chances of winning, you must not only know the proper strategies to follow for the machines you play, but you must use the strategies correctly. I will outline strategies for the different variations in this section. It will then be up to you to follow them and give the machines a run for your money.

Playing incorrect strategies or being unfamiliar with machines gives percentages back to the casino, and that is something you never want to do. Always play at your best and be prepared for the machines you will play. That gives you the best shot of walking away a winner.

General Strategy #5: Money Management

In any form of gambling, if you want to be a winner, you must make money management king. While every player knows this rule, few follow it. They don't even give themselves the chance to beat the casino. You must take money management seriously. There is an entire chapter in this book devoted to the subject. Read this chapter carefully and follow its advice.

Let's now move on to the individual games and the best strategies to follow for each one. Depending upon the ease of presentation, some strategies will be shown in chart form and others will just be written in descriptive form. We'll start with Jacks or Better, the original and still-popular form of video poker.

12. WINNING STRATEGY: JACKS OR BETTER

9-6 MACHINES

Since these machines are so popular, I'm showing the strategies with the explanations below and the charts as well.

1. Whenever you hold <u>four cards to a royal flush</u>, discard the fifth card, even if that card gives you a flush or pair.

2. Keep a <u>jacks or better pair</u> and any higher hand such as a three-of-a-kind or straight over three to the royal. Play the <u>three to a royal</u> over any lesser hand such as a low pair or four flush.

3. With <u>two cards to a royal</u>, keep four-straights, four-flushes, and high pairs or better instead. Otherwise, go for the royal.

4. Never break up a <u>straight or flush</u>, unless a one card draw gives you a chance for the royal.

5. Keep <u>jacks or better</u> over a four-straight or four-flush.

6. Never break up a <u>four-of-a-kind</u>, <u>full house</u>, <u>three-of-a-</u>

kind or two pair hand. The **rags**, worthless cards for the latter two hands, should be dropped on the draw.

7. Always keep the jacks or better pair, except when you have four cards to the royal or four to the straight flush.

8. Keep low pairs over the four-straight, but discard them in favor of the four-flushes and three or four to a royal flush.

9. When you're dealt unmade hands (a pre-draw hand with no payable combination of cards), save your hands in this order: four-to-a-royal flush and straight flush, three-to-a-royal flush, four-flushes, four-straights, three-to-a-straight flush, two-to-a-royal flush, two cards (jack or higher) and one card (jack or higher).

10. Lacking any of the above, with no card jack or higher, discard all the cards and draw five fresh ones.

A WORD ABOUT THE CHARTS

All strategy charts identify a payout schedule (as listed earlier) so you can identify the proper strategy to match up to the machines. The hands in all the strategy charts are listed in order of strength from the most powerful to the least powerful. When there is a choice of different types of hands that you can hold, always keep the hands listed high in the chart over the ones below them. For example, you'd always hold a three-of-a-kind over three-to-a-royal flush, so all charts will have three-of-a-kind listed higher in the chart.

Simplified Basic Strategy Chart

The following chart sums up the simplified basic strategy for Jacks or Better, 9-6 Machines. Note that you'll keep a high pair over a three-to-a-royal but throw it away in favor of a four-to-a-royal.

JACKS OR BETTER
Full Pay 9-6 Machine

Hand to be Held	Cards Held	Cards Drawn
Royal Flush	5	0
Straight Flush	5	0
Four-of-a-kind	5	0
Full House	5	0
Four-to-a-royal	4	1
Flush	5	0
Three-of-a-kind	3	2
Straight	5	0
Four-to-a-straight flush	4	1
Two Pair	4	1
High Pair	2	3
Three-to-a-royal	3	2
Four-to-a-flush	4	1
Low Pair	2	3
Four-to-a-straight	4	1
Three-to-a-straight flush	3	2
Two-to-a-royal	2	3
Two High Cards	2	3
One High Card	1	4
Garbage Hand	0	5

8-5 NON-PROGRESSIVE MACHINES

The cost of receiving only six coins for a full house and five for a flush for each coin played – as opposed to the nine and six respectively of the 9-6 machines – reduces the payback to 97.3%.

In a 8-5 non-progressive machine, where the royal pays only 4,000 coins, you would play the same exact strategy as in the 9-6 – with one exception. You'd hold two-to-a-royal flush over three-to-a-straight flush. The lesser pay of the flush possibility makes the royal draw more valuable. (The additional exception of keeping a high pair over three-to-a-royal draw, which is correct in the 8-5 Progressive version due to the higher royal flush payout, is not correct here.)

8-5 PROGRESSIVE MACHINES

The machine reset value for the royal flush usually starts at 5,000 coins ($1,250 on a 25¢ machine, $5,000 on a $1 machine) causing a few changes in our strategy as you'll see below. This change gives the machine a 1/2% better starting payback at 97.8%. The growing payouts for royal flushes add to the payback percentage to the point that a jackpot of about 6,800 coins brings the player to a 100% payback – no edge to the casino.

The 8-5 Jacks or Better Progressive chart (following page) is similar to the 9-6 chart except that more preference is given to the royal flush draws in two instances. When you hold both a high pair and three-to-a-royal flush, discard the pair in favor of the draw. Also, when you hold two-to-a-royal flush and three-to-a-straight flush simultaneously, keep the royal draw over the straight flush draw.

In the first case, the higher levels of the royal flush payout make the royal flush draws more valuable to play. In the second case, the factor of the weaker flush payout (five coins as opposed to six) contributes to the preference of playing the royal flush draw over the straight flush draw. Otherwise, the strategy is the same as the 9-6 chart.

JACKS OR BETTER
8-5 Progressive Machine

Hand to be Held	Cards Held	Cards Drawn
Royal Flush	5	0
Straight Flush	5	0
Four-of-a-kind	5	0
Full House	5	0
Four-to-a-royal	4	1
Flush	5	0
Three-of-a-kind	3	2
Straight	5	0
Four-to-a-straight flush	4	1
Two Pair	4	1
Three-to-a-royal	3	2
High Pair	2	3
Four-to-a-flush	4	1
Low Pair	2	3
Four-to-a-straight	4	1
Two-to-a-royal	2	3
Three-to-a-straight flush	3	2
Two High Cards	2	3
One High Card	1	4
Garbage Hand	0	5

BONUS QUAD MACHINES

There are many variations of the Bonus Quad machines, too many to cover all the possibilities. I showed the payback schedules earlier of a few popular IGT machines, including the Bonus Poker Deluxe, Double Bonus, and Double Double Bonus. In addition to these very popular IGT machines, you'll find many more variieties out there with a wide range of names and payout schedules.

However, the payout schedules are often similar enough that you can apply the strategies shown here.

BONUS POKER DELUXE & DOUBLE DOUBLE BONUS

The strategies for these two games are identical to the 9-6 machines. Refer to the 9-6 chart for the correct plays. One specific change that can be made, for players that want a more perfect strategy, is to play the hand J, Q, K, K, 5, as a three-to-a-royal flush in the Double Double Bonus game, and not as a high pair as indicated in the 9-6 strategy chart. The added possibilities of the two way straight (plus three high cards as opposed to a 10, J, Q), makes this a slightly better play. In the Bonus Poker Deluxe game though, the high pair is played over any three-to-a-royal.

DOUBLE BONUS POKER

The higher payout on the straight with the payout schedule shown – at five coins here, as opposed to four coins on the other quads above and the 9-6 and 8-5 machines – puts a little more emphasis on playing the straight draw. On this machine, the four-to-a-straight and the three-to-a-straight flush both get played over the low pair. The full payout schedule follows.

DOUBLE BONUS POKER 9-6 Payout		
Hand to be Held	**Cards Held**	**Cards Drawn**
Royal Flush	5	0
Straight Flush	5	0
Four-of-a-kind	5	0
Full House	5	0
Four-to-a-royal	4	1
Flush	5	0
Three-of-a-kind	3	2
Straight	5	0
Four-to-a-straight flush	4	1
Two Pair	4	1
High Pair	2	3
Three-to-a-royal	3	2
Four-to-a-flush	4	1
Four-to-a-straight	4	1
Three-to-a-straight flush	3	2
Low Pair	2	3
Two-to-a-royal	2	3
Two High Cards	2	3
One High Card	1	4
Garbage Hand	0	5

BONUS ROYAL

Like the Bonus Quads, there are many variations of Bonus Royal machines – too many to cover all the possibilities with the limited space I have in this book. However, the machines are often similar in strategy, if not exact in many cases, so the examples I show below may very well apply to similar machines you may find.

You pursue a different strategy in the Bonus Royal variations when you have a shot at getting the specified flush for the bonus. This will be indicated in the chart by using the letters "sp," short for *specified suit*. The strategy chart on the next page is for the payouts as shown earlier.

JACKS OR BETTER
Bonus Royal

Hand to be Held	Cards Held	Cards Drawn
Royal Flush	5	0
Straight Flush	5	0
Four-of-a-kind	5	0
Full House	5	0
Four-to-a-royal	4	1
Flush (sp)	5	0
Three-of-a-kind	3	2
Four-to-a-straight flush (sp)	4	1
Flush	5	0
Four-to-inside-straight flush (sp)	4	1
Straight	5	0
Four-to-straight flush	4	1
Three-to-a-royal (sp)	3	2
Two Pair	4	1
Four-to-inside-straight flush	4	1
Four-to-a-flush (sp)	4	1
Three-to-a-royal	3	2
High Pair	2	3
Four-to-a-flush	4	1
Three-to-a-straight flush (sp)	3	2
Low Pair	2	3
Four-to-a-straight	4	1
Two-to-a-royal (sp)	2	3
Three-to-a-straight flush	3	2
Two-to-a-royal	2	3
Two High Cards	2	3
One High Card	1	4
Garbage Hand	0	5

13. WINNING STRATEGY: TENS OR BETTER / TWO PAIR OR BETTER

Tens or Better is played just like Jacks or Better (you'll see that the strategy chart is identical), with the only exception being that a pair of 10s should be played and not discarded as in Jacks or Better. In the following chart, high cards refer to **J, Q, K, A**, and the **10**, and a high pair is any pair of 10s or higher.

In Two Pair or Better, not having any payout at all for a high pair removes the thinking of the high card, and the greater payouts given on flushes and straights (compared to the 9-6 Jacks or Better) dictates playing hands that you wouldn't play in regular Jacks or Better, such as two-to-a-flush and three-to-a-straight.

Take a look at the strategy charts for these two games on the next two pages.

TENS OR BETTER
Full Pay 6-5 Machine

Hand to be Held	Cards Held	Cards Drawn
Royal Flush	5	0
Straight Flush	5	0
Four-of-a-kind	5	0
Full House	5	0
Four-to-a-royal	4	1
Flush	5	0
Three-of-a-kind	3	2
Straight	5	0
Four-to-a-straight flush	4	1
Two Pair	4	1
High Pair (10s or better)	2	3
Three-to-a-royal	3	2
Four-to-a-flush	4	1
Low Pair	2	3
Four-to-a-straight	4	1
Three-to-a-straight flush	3	2
Two-to-a-royal	2	3
Two High Cards (10 or better)	2	3
One High Card (10 or better)	1	4
Garbage Hand	0	5

WINNING STRATEGY: TENS OR BETTER/ TWO PAIR OR BETTER

TWO PAIR OR BETTER
No Wild Cards - Full Pay

Hand to Be Held	Cards Held	Cards Drawn
Royal Flush	5	0
Straight Flush	5	0
Four-of-a-kind	5	0
Full House	5	0
Four-to-a-royal	4	1
Flush	5	0
Three-of-a-kind	3	2
Straight	5	0
Four-to-a-straight flush	4	1
Two Pair	4	1
Four-to-a-flush	4	1
Three-to-a-royal	3	2
Any Pair	2	3
Three-to-a-straight flush	3	2
Four-to-a-straight (one gap)	4	1
Three-to-a-flush	3	2
Two-to-a-royal	2	3
Three-to-a-straight	3	2
Two-to-a-straight flush	2	3
Two-to-a-flush	2	3
Garbage Hand	0	5

14. WINNING STRATEGY: WILD CARD VARIETIES

JOKER WILD: ACE-KING

In the Ace-King version of Joker Wild: Two Pair, a pair of kings or aces gives a payout; thus we consider the ace and king as high cards and a pair of either one as a high pair.

JOKER WILD
Ace-King

JOKER HELD

Hand to be Held	Cards Held	Cards Drawn
Five-of-a-kind	5	0
Royal Flush	5	0
Straight Flush	5	0
Four-of-a-kind	4	1
Full House	5	0
Four-to-a-royal	4	1
Flush	5	0
Four-to-a-straight flush	4	1
Straight	5	0
Three-of-a-kind	3	2
Four-to-a-flush	4	1

Three-to-a-royal flush	3	2
Three-to-a-straight flush	3	2
High Pair (Kings or Aces)	2	3
Four-to-a-flush	4	1
Four-to-a-straight	4	1
Joker	1	4

NO JOKER

Hand to be Held	Cards Held	Cards Drawn
Royal Flush	5	0
Straight Flush	5	0
Four-to-a-royal	4	1
Four-of-a-kind	4	1
Full House	5	0
Flush	5	0
Four-to-a-straight flush	4	1
Straight	5	0
Three-of-a-kind	3	2
Two Pairs	4	1
Three-to-a-royal	3	2
High Pair (Kings or Aces)	2	3
Four-to-a-flush	4	1
Pair of 2s-Queens	2	3
Three-to-a-straight flush	3	2
Four-to-a-straight	4	1
Two-to-a-royal	2	3
Ace and King	2	3
High Card (Ace or King)	1	4
Garbage Hand	0	5

JOKER WILD: TWO PAIR

There are two strategy charts below: one for hands when no joker is held, and one when a joker is held. You'll note that in the joker chart that there is no listing for two pair – that's because the hand would actually be three-of-a-kind! For example, if you held joker, 6, 9, 9, 4, you would keep the two 9s and the joker for three 9s, and not the 6 also for two pair. That would be a weaker hand.

JOKER WILD		
Two Pair		
JOKER HELD		
Hand to be Held	**Cards Held**	**Cards Drawn**
Five-of-a-kind	5	0
Royal Flush	5	0
Straight Flush	5	0
Four-of-a-kind	4	1
Full House	5	0
Flush	5	0
Four-to-a-royal	4	1
Four-to-a-straight flush	4	1
Straight	5	0
Three-of-a-kind	3	2
Three-to-a-royal flush	3	2
Three-to-a-straight flush	3	2
Four-to-a-flush	4	1
Four-to-a-straight	4	1
Three-to-a-straight	3	2
Joker	1	4

NO JOKER (cont'd)

Hand to be Held	Cards Held	Cards Drawn
Royal Flush	5	0
Straight Flush	5	0
Four-to-a-royal	4	1
Four-of-a-kind	4	1
Full House	5	0
Flush	5	0
Straight	5	0
Three-of-a-kind	3	2
Four-to-a-straight flush	4	1
Two Pairs	4	1
Three-to-a-royal	3	2
Four-to-a-flush	4	1
Four-to-a-straight	4	1
Three-to-a-straight flush	3	2
One Pair	2	3
Four-to-a-straight (1 gap)	4	1
Three-to-a-flush	3	2
Two-to-a-royal	2	3
Three-to-a-straight	3	2
Two-to-a-straight flush	2	3
Garbage Hand	0	5

DEUCES WILD

Deuces are extremely valuable cards, so when you get them, make sure you never discard them by accident. You'll notice that there is no payoff for hands less than three-of-a-kind, so your strategy must be adjusted accordingly.

The key in Deuces Wild, as in the non-wild versions, is to go for the big payout – the royal flush. Therefore, when you have three cards toward a royal flush, discard the other two and go for it. Of course, the same holds true when you have four-to-the-royal. Thus, if you have two deuces and a 10 or higher, along with two under-10 cards of no value, go for the royal.

Similarly, if you have two deuces and three cards below the 10 in value, dump the three cards and hang onto the deuces, unless two of the cards are paired – in that case you have four of a kind – or if the two cards retained give you four cards toward a straight flush. If you hold one or two deuces with nothing else that's interesting, dump the junk and hang onto the deuces. If your hand is really poor, and you're dealt five unrelated cards, get rid of them all and go for five fresh ones.

Three-card flushes or straights are worthless in this game, as are single unmatched high cards. Discard these hands. You should also get rid of two pair hands – they don't pay. Hang onto one of the pairs and go for three new cards.

If one of the pairs is teamed with a wild deuce, keep the three-of-a-kind. However, if the deuce forms a high pair, it does no good at all. As suggested above, keep the deuce and draw four new cards.

Keep a pair at the outset, unless you've got a three-card royal flush. In that case you'll dump the pair and go for the gold. You'll find that many of the hands you'll be dealt will contain nothing worth saving, and you'll be drawing for five fresh cards. Three-card straights and flushes fit in this category, along with some of the others I've mentioned. In any case, don't be afraid to discard your original five cards if you hold nothing of value.

It'll take a little while to get used to wild card video poker after playing the non-wild versions, but once you get accustomed, you should have a lot of fun at these machines.

DEUCES WILD
Full Pay Machine

__NO DEUCES__

Hand to be Held	Cards Held	Cards Drawn
Royal Flush	5	0
Four-to-a-royal	4	1
Straight Flush	5	0
Four-of-a-kind	4	1
Full House	5	0
Flush	5	0
Straight	5	0
Three-of-a-kind	3	2
Four-to-a-straight flush	4	1
Three-to-a-royal	3	2
One Pair (discard second pair)	2	3
Four-to-a-flush	4	1
Four-to-a-straight	4	1
Three-to-a-straight flush	3	2
Two-to-a-royal	2	3
Garbage Hand	0	5

ONE DEUCE (cont'd)

Hand to be Held	Cards Held	Cards Drawn
Royal Flush	5	0
Five-of-a-kind	5	0
Straight Flush	5	0
Four-of-a-kind	4	1
Four-to-a-royal	4	1
Full House	5	0
Three-of-a-kind	3	2
Four-to-a-straight flush	4	1
Flush	5	0
Straight	5	0
Three-to-a-royal	3	2
One Deuce	1	4

TWO DEUCES

Hand to be Held	Cards Held	Cards Drawn
Royal Flush	5	0
Five-of-a-kind	5	0
Straight Flush	5	0
Four-of-a-kind	4	1
Four-to-a-royal	4	1
Two Deuces	2	3

THREE DEUCES

Hand to be Held	Cards Held	Cards Drawn
Royal Flush	5	0
Five-of-a-kind	5	0
Three Deuces	3	2

FOUR DEUCES

Hand to be Held	Cards Held	Cards Drawn
Four Deuces	4	1

DEUCES WILD PROGRESSIVE

Following are the strategy charts for the Progressive Deuces Wild game.

DEUCES WILD PROGRESSIVE
Full Pay

<u>NO DEUCES</u>

Hand to Be Held	Cards Held	Cards Drawn
Royal Flush	5	0
Four-to-a-royal	4	1
Straight Flush	5	0
Four-of-a-kind	4	1
Full House	5	0
Flush	5	0
Straight	5	0
Three-of-a-kind	3	2
Four-to-a-straight flush	4	1
Three-to-a-royal	3	2
Four-to-a-flush	4	1
Two Pair	4	1
One Pair	2	3
Four-to-a-straight	4	1
Three-to-a-straight flush	3	2
Two-to-a-royal	2	3
Garbage Hand	0	5

ONE DEUCE (cont'd)

Hand to be Held	Cards Held	Cards Drawn
Royal Flush	5	0
Five-of-a-kind	5	0
Straight Flush	5	0
Four-of-a-kind	4	1
Four-to-a-royal	4	1
Full House	5	0
Flush	5	0
Four-to-a-straight flush	4	1
Straight	5	0
Three-of-a-kind	3	2
Three-to-a-royal	3	2
Three-to-a-straight flush	3	2
One Deuce	1	4

TWO DEUCES

Hand to be Held	Cards Held	Cards Drawn
Royal Flush	5	0
Five-of-a-kind	5	0
Straight Flush	5	0
Four-of-a-kind	4	1
Four-to-a-royal	4	1
Four-to-a-straight flush	4	1
Two Deuces	2	3

THREE DEUCES

Hand to be Held	Cards Held	Cards Drawn
Royal Flush	5	0
Five-of-a-kind	5	0
Three Deuces	3	2

FOUR DEUCES (cont'd)		
Hand to be Held	**Cards Held**	**Cards Drawn**
Four Deuces	4	1

DEUCES AND JOKER WILD

With five wild cards, four deuces and a joker, running around the deck, you'll get all sorts of interesting hands. You'll need to be familiar with the different strategy tables that follow; the no wild card hands, and the hands with the different numbers of wild cards.

DEUCES AND JOKER WILD Full Pay		
NO WILD CARDS		
Hand to Be Held	**Cards Held**	**Cards Drawn**
Royal Flush	5	0
Four-to-a-royal	4	1
Straight Flush	5	0
Four-of-a-kind	4	1
Full House	5	0
Flush	5	0
Straight	5	0
Three-of-a-kind	3	2
Four-to-a-straight flush	4	1
Three-to-a-royal	3	2
Four-to-a-flush	4	1
Three-to-a-straight flush	3	2
Two Pairs	4	1
One Pair	2	3
Four-to-a-straight	4	1
Garbage Hand	0	5

ONE WILD CARD (cont'd)

Hand to be Held	Cards Held	Cards Drawn
Royal Flush	5	0
Five-of-a-kind	5	0
Straight Flush	5	0
Four-of-a-kind	4	1
Full House	5	0
Flush	5	0
Four-to-a-royal	4	1
Straight	5	0
Four-to-a-straight flush	4	1

ONE WILD CARD

Hand to be Held	Cards Held	Cards Drawn
Three-of-a-kind	3	2
Three-to-a-royal	3	2
Three-to-a-straight flush	3	2
Four-to-a-flush	4	1
Four-to-a -straight	4	1
One Wild Card	1	4

TWO WILD CARDS

Hand to be Held	Cards Held	Cards Drawn
Royal Flush	5	0
Five-of-a-kind	5	0
Straight Flush	5	0
Four-of-a-kind	4	1
Four-to-a-royal	4	1
Flush	5	0
Four-to-a-straight flush	4	1
Two Wild Cards	2	3

THREE WILD CARDS (cont'd)

Hand to be Held	Cards Held	Cards Drawn
Royal Flush	5	0
Five-of-a-kind	5	0
Three Wild Cards	3	2

FOUR WILD CARDS

Hand to be Held	Cards Held	Cards Drawn
Four Deuces	4	1
Three Deuces and Joker	4	1

FIVE WILD CARDS

Hand to be Held	Cards Held	Cards Drawn
Five Wild Cards	5	0

15. WINNING STRATEGY: MULTIPLE DECK AND SPECIALTY VARIETIES

TRIPLE PLAY

Triple Play poker is really Jacks or Better – that is, it's three Jacks or Better games rolled into one. The correct strategy to follow here is identical to the one to follow in Jacks or Better games with the same paytables.

At the Triple Play machines, you need to keep in mind that the greater number of coins you play per round, the greater the volatility of your bankroll. One loss at this machine is three times greater than at a regular machine when you're playing the max number of coins – that's fifteen coins. Of course, one win can be three times as great as well (or more) if all three hands offer a payout, but you must always consider the basic concept of money management when you wager your money in a casino.

FIVE-DECK POKER & FIVE-DECK FRENZY

The strategies for these five-deck varieties are beyond the scope of this book. Remember that I did show the basic concepts of the games earlier so that you understand how they are played.

SECRETS OF WINNING VIDEO POKER

DOUBLE DOWN VIDEO POKER

Talk about a tough game to beat – this is it. I don't recommend this variation at all. It's one long uphill battle. Unlike the other video poker variations, where you can discard up to five cards and get five new ones, here you get only five cards total – that's it. You have no opportunities to draw new cards. Whatever you get dealt is the hand you keep.

The interesting twist on this game is the doubling feature. That makes for a lot of fun when the first four cards you're dealt are winners. And unlike in the Jacks or Better games, the minimum winning combination is only a pair of 6s. But don't let that fool you into thinking it is easier to get winning combinations than the jacks minimum in Jacks or Better. In Jacks or Better you get a chance to draw multiple cards to improve. In Double Down, you must get a winner in the first five cards you draw. That makes for stretches of over ten hands sometimes when you can't buy a winner of any sort and the only pair you make at all is of the 5s and 3s sort – the ones that pay you nothing.

The strategies for this game are fairly simple. You're dealt four cards and have to decide, based on their values, whether they are worth a doubling of the bet. The first obvious choice is to keep all hands that are automatic winners. Thus any pair of 6s or higher (remember this is not Jacks or Better), two pair, and three- or four-of-a-kind are automatically doubled.

No matter what the fifth card is, you can't lose. And with any hand of jacks or higher, you're effectively doubling the winnings. Additionally, you also have the chance that the fifth card will improve the hand further for a larger payout – and the payout is again doubled. (If the pairs of 6s through 10s don't improve, since they pay back only what you put in the machine, the doubling of the bet returns the same even money anyway.)

What hands should you double in addition to the automatic winners?

Four-to-a-straight flush and four-to-a-royal flush are definite doublers. You want extra money out on those hands if you should be so fortunate as to get four cards lined up like that. The other two hands worth doubling are four-to-a-flush and four-to-a-straight. Double these only if the four-straight is consecutive, such as 5 6 7 8. You would not double 5 6 7 9 – your chances of catching the four 8s to fill are exactly half your chances of catching the four 4s and 9s of the 5 6 7 8 hand. I'll show this in chart form.

DOUBLE YOUR BET IF YOU HOLD:
Any paying combination (6s or higher)
Four-to-a-royal flush
Four-to-a-straight flush
Four-to-a-flush
Four-to-a-consecutive straight

If you're winning, you'll have fun playing this game. The likelihood, though, is that you won't be winning. Instead, you'll be chasing your money.

DOUBLE CARD JACKS OR BETTER

At first glance, the doubled card Jacks or Better variation sounds attractive. But if you look at the game more carefully, you'll soon see that the doubled card feature offered here is anything but good. In fact, when you get the doubled card, your chances of getting a winning hand are actually *reduced*.

The doubled card in this variation should not be confused with a wild card. This doubled card adds nothing to your chances of winning, and in fact, when you hold it, it effectively reduces your hand to only a four card hand! For example, if you draw one card to a four-flush, and receive the double card as the draw, you're out and have won nothing.

This 53rd card, when held, spells doom for any flush, straight, straight flush or royal flush hand if it is drawn, kills any chances for a full house, and reduces the possibility of every other hand's improving to a larger hand. For example, say you're drawing one card to a four straight. Rather than the normal 8 chances in 47 of a 52-card deck, the 53rd card makes it now 8 chances in 48, around a 2% more difficult situation.

The same worsening odds hold true for flushes, straight flushes, royal flushes, and even pairs, where the extra card in the deck makes for one more card that will not make the hand. In essence, the doubled card is like a dead card that is added to the deck. It's useful only in increasing payoffs if a hand is already made, and at the same time it decreases that hand's potential to become a stronger hand.

WINNING STRATEGY: MULTIPLE DECK/ SPECIALTY VARIETIES

The doubled card game offers you terrible odds, and you should avoid it. If you do decide to play, there are some basic strategy ideas you should keep in mind. First, if you're dealt the doubled card, discard it unless you already have a made hand – that is, one that gives you an automatic payoff. Thus, you'll keep the doubled card with a jacks or better pair, two pair, three-of-a-kind, and four-of-a-kind. On these hands, the doubled card will double your payoff.

But in all other situations, where the doubled card is not combined with an automatic winner, discard it. You want to get an extra card to improve your chances of making a hand. When the doubled card is not in your original holding, play the same strategy as Jacks or Better.

PICK FIVE

Pick Five is a tough game to beat. Compared to standard Jacks or Better games, where you make playing decisions based on a full five-card hand, the one card at a time decision-making involved here reduces your chances of drawing winning hands.

It won't take you long in front of this machine to realize that winning hands are coming infrequently, and that you would prefer games with more positive reinforcement. Meanwhile, let's look at some strategy tips to make your play more efficient.

Tips for the First Card

On the first two cards dealt, always choose a jack-ace card over any other card. If you pair it, your hand will achieve an automatic payoff.

If you are dealt two high cards, keep the jack over any other high card. Your second choice should be the queen, because it gives you slightly more chances to catch a straight than others do. For example, if the second card is a queen, and the third card is a 7, 8, 9 or 10, your choice of the jack as the first card will prove more valuable in leaving your chances open for a straight than if you had held a king. In the latter case, the 10 is the only non-pairing third card that will keep the chances for a straight open.

A jack is also better than the ace, because if the second card is a high card (which you should always choose over a 2, 3, 4, or 5 – the other four cards that could potentially form a straight with the ace), then the possibility of the straight is more likely for the same reasons stated above.

If you're dealt two medium cards, such as a 9 and a 6, choose the 9 for the possible straight possibilities down the line. You should also choose the 9 over a card such as the 3 or 4. Since you'll always be choosing high cards – jacks to aces – to be kept over low cards, you leave yourself open to more straight possibilities by keeping 10s, 9s, and even 8s, over, 2s-6s.

Tips for the Second Card
Once you have established your first card, your highest priority is to pair that card. A card that pairs the first card, even as a low pair, is better than a card which makes a straight, a flush, a straight flush, or even a royal flush possible. Always take the pair when you have that opportunity.

Pick a high card – jack to ace – over any other card, including ones that form possible straights, flushes, straight flushes, or royal flushes (such as a 10). Having just two cards toward those straights or flushes is too speculative. You're better off with a high card that can win if you pair it.

Tips for the Third Card

As on the second card, choose a pair over straight or flush possibilities. For example, if you hold J 5 of hearts, and you can pick from either a 7 of hearts or a 5 of spades, take the 5 for the pair. Obviously, if one of those choices was a jack of any suit instead of the 5, you should pick the jack.

If you already have a pair and the third card can give you three-of-a-kind, play the trips. Obviously this is a no-brainer. If a pair cannot be formed, your next best option is to choose a high card, if one appears. For example, if you hold A 4, and the choice is jack or 7, pick the jack. You're always looking to create opportunities for paying hands.

Tips for the Fourth Card

Picks that give you four-of-a-kind, three-of-a-kind, and two pair hands are always your best choice. If the fourth card gives you four-to-a-straight flush, choose that over a pair. Play a high pair over a four-flush or four-straight, but if the pair is low (10s or lower), play the four-flush and four-straight instead.

If you have none of the above, pick the card that forms a pair, particularly if it is a high pair. Without a pair choice, choose four-straights and four-flushes over a high card, and choose a high card over a low card if no other paying combinations are present.

Tips for the Fifth Card

Fifth card strategy is easy. Obviously, you'll pick the card that gives you the highest paying hand.

ALTERNATE PROGRESSIVE METERS

As we have seen, there are many forms of video poker variations. New shades and colors of this game seem to appear all the time. You'll sometimes find dual progressive jackpots, where an arrow alternately points from one jackpot and then back to the next. If one jackpot is high and attractive and the other is very low and unattractive, you can pursue a strategy of playing the full five coins when the high jackpot is in play and playing just one coin on the alternate hand when the low jackpot is in play.

SUMMARY OF WINNING STRATEGY

Video poker is certainly a fun game, for it is a game of skill. As I stated in the beginning, if you play properly, you can have the edge over the casino. As with blackjack, you'll need to study the correct strategies carefully to come out a winner.

For those players who are serious about winning money at video poker, I highly recommend the professional video poker strategy advertised in the back of this book. You'll learn the important differences in strategy between the 8-5 Progressive and 9-6 Jacks or Better machines, and you'll receive complete strategy charts for these games, the wild card games, and others.

Meanwhile, use your skill to good advantage, and see if you can beat the house and be a winner!

SECTION D
-MORE KNOWLEDGE-

16. SLOTS CLUBS

The slots clubs are the best way for video poker and slots players to amass a seemingly endless supply of room comps, meal comps, show comps, line passes, and even cash rebates. In fact, if you play your "reels" right, you can virtually enjoy free vacations doing just what you like to do best in the casinos – playing the machines! And that's not bad at all.

Given the large profits casinos earn from their machine players and their recognition of the importance of the revenue these gamblers generate, you, as a video poker and slots player today, are king. No longer are the table games the real bread and butter of a casino. It's the new era of the machines, the gambling technology revolution. Video poker and slots machines now comprise well more than 50% of a typical casino's action!

Casinos rely more and more on their video poker and slots players to generate bottom line profits, and they have steadily increased the space allocated to machines to reflect this. Now, anywhere you go in a modern casino, you see them, you hear them, you *feel* them. As fast as their presence expands, new players expand with them, plopping those coins into the bellies of the one armed beasts.

SECRETS OF WINNING VIDEO POKER

Slots and video poker players are no longer taken for granted. With revenues in the billions, that's right, *billions*, worldwide, casinos are realizing who their important players really are and are actively pursuing their patronage. Comps, incentives, and bonuses, once reserved for table players, are now in the full domain of machine players.

That's great news for video poker players, because casinos are now motivated to get you to their machines as opposed to their competitors' machines. I'll show you how to take advantage of this situation to your full benefit.

ABOUT THE SLOTS CLUBS

Slots clubs are basically enrollment programs that players sign up for as members. There is no charge to join, but lots of benefits from doing so. The concept is simple. Once a player enrolls as a member, the casino will issue a member card with the player's name and card number. When you insert your card into a machine prior to playing, it automatically tracks your betting action. The more action you give the casino, the greater the benefits you enjoy just for playing the machines. And what could be better?

For example, in some casinos, you can accrue enough credits after approximately just one hour of action at the $1 machines – or 2-3 hours at the 25¢ machines – that you can qualify for benefits. Benefits and comps are all a function of the amount of money you play. And that, in casino parlance, is called **action**. Action, to a casino, is not some theoretical concept. It's the total amount of money played.

For example, if you're playing $1 video poker, five coins at a time, and play 500 spins, you've given the casino $2,500 worth of action (500 spins at $5 each). If you're playing quarters, five at a time to a machine, and you play 1,000 spins, your action is equal to 5,000 quarters, or $1,250.

Note that the action given to a machine or a casino is not measured by how much you've won or lost. It's measured by the total amount of plays multiplied by the amount you bet. Thus, using the above example at the $1 machines, whether you've won $115 or lost $115 overall, to the casino, your action is still that same $1,500. Plenty good to start earning comps, and really good if you've got a $115 profit to show as well.

And that's why slots clubs are so great. If you're going to be playing the machines anyway, you're guaranteed "winnings," so to speak, by dint of the simple fact that your action is earning rewards. For example, if you're playing the 25¢ slots for several hours, and you drop $23 at the machines, but you earn two free $15 dinner comps, you won't feel so bad. You've come out ahead of the game.

These slots cards are great tracking devices that not only record a player's **total action** – the total amount of money wagered at the machine – but also keep track of a player's behavior. The casinos want to better understand their customers, the machines they like to play and in what denominations, and how long they play each machine. Each casino has its own slots program, some with greater benefits than others. But all are worth joining if you plan to play slots at a casino, and especially if you plan on playing a lot of slots.

SECRETS OF WINNING VIDEO POKER

Slots clubs began as an experiment at the Sands Casino in Atlantic City in 1982. The Sands Casino wanted to attract and keep slots players there. In 1984, the Golden Nugget introduced this concept to Las Vegas, and as they say, the rest is history. Almost every casino today in Las Vegas or Atlantic City has an actively promoted slots club. The few that don't are at a tremendous marketing disadvantage. After all, why would serious slots or video poker players patronize a casino offering nothing special to attract their play when the casino next door has a great slots club with tons of inducements? The answer is simple – they wouldn't.

While the casinos are eager to induce players with attractive slots club benefits, the players are just as eager to reap the rewards for doing what they were going to do anyway – play the machines. The trick is learning how to play the system to maximize your rewards.

SHOULD YOU JOIN A SLOTS CLUB?

Absolutely! If you're going to be playing video poker, you should definitely join. You have nothing to lose and everything to gain. There is no membership price or cost of any type to be a member. Outside of the few minutes it might take to do the application process that gets you going – which is nothing more than getting your basic information – the membership has nothing to do with income level or credit information. There is no other effort you must make to enjoy the many benefits.

Some players feel that they don't bet enough even to bother signing up. *Au contraire*. It's not how much you're willing to risk at the tables, it's the amount of action you give those machines that counts. Well, you might say, I'm only going to play with $20. That $20 may earn you $50, $100, or more in comps if your luck is good.

Let's say you get on a roll with that $20 and work it for several hours or more of play before walking away with $22, for $2 in profit. Or let's just say that the machine swallowed up that $20. Either way, you've possibly generated enough action to activate some comps. In total, if you added up all the bets you made during that playing session, it will perhaps have added up to hundreds of dollars in action. That's a lot more significant than the mere $20 you thought you were wagering. *The actual action was much higher than the actual wager.*

Many players don't realize this, and they lose out on benefits they otherwise could have accumulated.

GETTING STARTED

Joining a slots club is as easy as filling out an application form. The Slots Hosts are usually located in the rear of the casinos, but if you can't find them, ask any of the personnel. They can probably send you in the right direction. I usually find that the security guards are the best employees to ask, especially in casinos that have a security officer posted at a central desk near the cashier.

The application process for joining is simple and the application itself won't take you long to fill out. The casinos are mostly concerned that they can properly identify you (they'll require a valid ID) and get you on their mailing list to keep you abreast of the latest and most exciting developments from their slots club.

Keep in mind that this application is simply a formality – nobody is going to get turned down. They have no interest in your credit history or how much money you make. This is not a credit application, only an application to get you going as a slots member.

CHOOSING THE BEST SLOTS CLUBS

In the beginning, getting the most for your gambling buck is a matter of researching the various casinos you're interested in and finding out who has the most generous incentives to get your business. Many casinos will give you a printed schedule showing how the rewards work. Comparing the different programs for their benefits is the best way to decide on what's right for you. This is the leg work, so to speak, that you'll need to do as you're getting established among the various clubs.

Some clubs won't give you any information at all. In fact, they may claim they don't know the structure of their point system. You should certainly avoid these casinos.

The real way to get going with the slots clubs and reap the maximum benefits is to join them all, or at least as many as you can. This doesn't mean you have to play in all of them. You should focus your playing in the clubs with the best machines and the best rewards. You'll be on all these clubs' mailing lists, and when there is a great slots promotion, you'll be the first to know. These casinos know that they have a lot of competition and they want to get you in their door. That means they need to give you big-time incentives to make your next trip to their casino.

With offers galore coming in, you can start cherry-picking the best deals. And you're on your way to all the freebies Las Vegas has to offer. With some good timing and a little luck, you may even find yourself with a free vacation - rooms, meals, shows, cash rebates, and even more points built up for more comps.

GETTING STARTED ON THE COMPS

Often, as soon as you sign up for a slots club, the casino will issue you freebies and incentives as your sign-up bonus. These may include meal or show discounts or comps, tee shirts, or bonus plays – really anything at all the casino is using as a promotion to get you to sign up for its club. These incentives frequently change with the moods and thinking of the promotions people, but if nothing else, they're an attractive way to get started when they're available.

The first thing that happens when you sign up for a slots club is that you'll be issued a card. This card identifies you as a player and member of the slots club which issued it. It will be used to track your play at the machines. And then you're ready to go. The casinos will have you on file and in the system. Armed with this card, you'll earn rewards credits every time you play.

Step one to insuring at least some promotional offers is to put that card to use right away with a little action in the casino. This lets the casinos know that they have a "live" player. It will make them work that much harder to pile you with incentives.

But even if you don't use your card right away in a casino's machines, the casino will have you down on its mailing list and will still entice you with offers through the mail. The figuring here, as with any mailing list, is that you're an interested player. With the right offer and the right timing, the casino may get you back in its doors to play more. If you're planning a trip to Vegas and a casino sends you some comp food tickets to get you in the door, that strategy just might work to everyone's benefit.

Some slots clubs may want to qualify their players – that is, they want to make sure you're really a *player,* one who is going to give them action and has proven so by already playing, not just someone who shows up on any list that he or she can get on. Or perhaps casinos may give the qualified players better offers. In any case, slots clubs change their thinking and offers all the time, depending upon their marketing programs, but we find that giving the card at least a little play is the safest way to get the ball rolling.

The next step toward really qualifying yourself as a *player* is to meet the casino's minimum level of play toward its first qualifying level. Again, the minimum playing requirements vary from casino to casino and can vary from one month to another as policies and the competitive environment changes. You'll have to see where things stand if you've been away from the casinos for a while and if what was a good program last time is still good, or if you find a slots club you like even better for this trip. Casino marketing programs are always in a flux.

Casinos that really value you as a customer will let you

know up front what they expect from you to earn these playing rewards. It will be spelled out in black and white just how much action you need to generate for the awards programs to kick in. Some casinos publish newsletters which will give you the ins and outs of the promotional details, and some might have that information verbally, while the less inspired casinos will keep all this a dark secret and, of course, generate less action from players who don't know what they can expect from their patronage.

Typically, and again this varies completely from one program to another, approximately one hour worth of action at the $1 slots (or 2-3 hours at the 25¢ machines) will kick in the first tier of bonuses and comps. Faster players may reach these levels a little faster; slower players may take a little longer. The critical element the casinos are looking for is the amount of action – how much money is wagered into the machines – not how long you happen to be sitting in front of a machine warming a chair.

The casinos want *action*. You give it to them, and they'll kick back to you with their incentives.

HOW THE SLOTS CARD WORKS

The most important factor in earning your full playing credits at the slot machines is to use your slots card. Every slot and video poker machine in the casino has a card reader that will accept your club card for play. These are typically found in the front of the machines, though they may be on the sides. The new IGT series of machines, the most prevalent machines on the market, contain their readers right in front, so they're easy for the player to see.

SECRETS OF WINNING VIDEO POKER

If, for some reason, you can't find the reader, or have trouble inserting your card into it, or have any other problem, call over one of the slots personnel. They'll be glad to help you get set up. That's why they're there.

Your first move, when you approach a machine and ready yourself for play, is to insert your card into the card reader. Upon its insertion, the card will usually trigger a greeting that identifies you by name, though sometimes the casino may have a theme greeting instead.

WHAT IF YOU LOSE YOUR CARD?
If you've left your card back home or in your hotel room, or even if you've lost it altogether, no problem. Go to the slots host. He'll give you a replacement card when you present your ID. This happens to players all the time. Casinos will be only too happy to set you up again with your card and get you back to the machines.

EARNING THE FIRST LEVEL OF SLOTS CLUB BENEFITS
Once you know the minimal levels of play you need to meet to qualify for the program's first level of benefits, the only variables that affect the time it takes to get to that first benefit level are the speed of your play (how many spins on average you play per hour) and the average number of coins you play per spin. To put both of those variables together, in essence, the formula boils down to how many coins you play per hour. The more coins you play per hour, the faster you accumulate the action required by a casino

to reach activation levels.

How do the casinos determine this first level? First we must understand how casinos rate a player's slots action in general, and then how they reward that action.

Casinos generally rate a player's action on a point system – they award so many points for each level of dollars played. You may receive one point per dollar played, one point per twenty dollars played, or even ten points per one dollar played. But none of this means anything unless you know what these points mean. Each point earned is relative to the value given it by that particular casino.

Each casino has its own point or earning system and activation levels, and it is only by knowing these levels that you can make sense of which program is good and which one is not quite as attractive. For example, getting ten points for one dollar won't mean anything if the activation level for this casino requires you to spend twice as much time playing your preferred denomination machine as another casino.

In other words, 1,000 points at one casino may be of more value to you than 1,000 points at a different one. 1,000 points at one casino may even be of more value than 10,000 points at another casino that throws points around.

There are other ways that casinos rate a player's action at their slots, but typically speaking, casinos will use the total dollar value action wagered by the player. The total number of coins placed into the machines multiplied by their dollar value is the most accurate and fair measure of play anyway. Playing three dollars a spin and spinning the reels 300 times yields an exact amount of action - $900. Another player may spend just as much time at that machine but put in only one third as much play.

Obviously, the first player is more valuable to the casino and is a player the casinos want to encourage even more than the second.

Casinos don't want to reward players just for spending time at a machine. Then players could just sit there soaking in the free drinks and the atmosphere, and accruing points with little play. Casinos want action, and there is no better measure of that action than adding up the coins played.

POINT EXPIRATION

Much like some frequent flier miles on the airlines, your points can expire if you haven't returned to a casino within twelve months of your last visit. You'll have to check with your slots host to find out if this may apply to you. If so, make sure to redeem any awards before they expire.

On the following pages, I've put together five Action Charts that show the amount of time you have to play at different denomination machines to accrue different amounts of play at a casino.

ACTION CHART - $1,000

Coin	Coins Played	Speed of Play	
		Fast	**Slow**
5¢	5	10 hours	11 hours
	3	16 hours	18 hours
	1	50 hours	60 hours
25¢	5	2 hours	2.5 hours
	3	3.5 hours	4 hours
	1	10 hours	12 hours
$1	5	30 minutes	45 minutes
	3	45 minutes	1 hour
	1	2.5 hours	3 hours
$5	5	6 minutes	7 minutes
	3	9 minutes	11 minutes
	1	30 minutes	37 minutes

This chart shows approximately how long it would take to reach **$1,000** in action. It does not take into account the house payback (return percentage) since it is only tracking the number of bets multiplied by the size of the bet. Keep in mind that this chart is only an approximation and that every individual's speed is different.

You see by the chart that the fewer coins played per pull, the longer it takes to reach the level shown. Similarly, the slower the player's average playing speed, the longer it will take.

Since the average player will play the full number of coins allowed by the machine, and the experienced player tends to go at faster paces, you can expect that the action levels will be hit more often at the faster pace.

ACTION CHART - $2,000

Coin	Coins Played	Speed of Play	
		Fast	Slow
5¢	5	20 hours	22.5 hours
	3	32.5 hours	37.5 hours
	1	100 hours	120 hours
25¢	5	4 hours	4.5 hours
	3	6.5 hours	7.5 hours
	1	20 hours	24 hours
$1	5	1 hour	1.5 hours
	3	1.5 hours	2 hours
	1	5 hours	6 hours
$5	5	12 minutes	14 minutes
	3	19 minutes	22 minutes
	1	1 hour	1.25 hours

This chart shows approximately how long it would take to reach **$2,000** in action. It does not take into account the house payback (return percentage) since it is only tracking the number of bets multiplied by the size of the bet. Keep in mind that this chart is only an approximation and that every individual's speed is different.

You see by the chart that the fewer coins played per pull, the longer it takes to reach the level shown. Similarly, the slower the player's average playing speed, the longer it will take.

Since the average player will play the full number of coins allowed by the machine, and the experienced player tends to go at faster paces, you can expect that the action levels will be hit more often at the faster pace.

ACTION CHART - $3,000

Coin	Coins Played	Speed of Play	
		Fast	Slow
5¢	5	30 hours	34 hours
	3	48 hours	57 hours
	1	150 hours	180 hours
25¢	5	6 hours	7 hours
	3	9 hours	11.5 hours
	1	30 hours	36 hours
$1	5	1.5 hour	2.25 hours
	3	2.25 hours	3 hours
	1	7.5 hours	9 hours
$5	5	18 minutes	21 minutes
	3	28 minutes	33 minutes
	1	1.5 hours	2 hours

This chart shows approximately how long it would take to reach **$3,000** in action. It does not take into account the house payback (return percentage) since it is only tracking the number of bets multiplied by the size of the bet. Keep in mind that this chart is only an approximation and that every individual's speed is different.

You see by the chart that the fewer coins played per pull, the longer it takes to reach the level shown. Similarly, the slower the player's average playing speed, the longer it will take.

Since the average player will play the full number of coins allowed by the machine, and the experienced player tends to go at faster paces, you can expect that the action levels will be hit more often at the faster pace.

ACTION CHART - $4,000

Coin	Coins Played	Speed of Play	
		Fast	**Slow**
5¢	5	40 hours	45 hours
	3	65 hours	75 hours
	1	200 hours	240 hours
25¢	5	8 hours	9 hours
	3	13 hours	15 hours
	1	40 hours	48 hours
$1	5	2 hours	3 hours
	3	3 hours	4 hours
	1	10 hours	12 hours
$5	5	24 minutes	28 minutes
	3	38 minutes	44 minutes
	1	2 hours	2.5 hours

This chart shows approximately how long it would take to reach **$4,000** in action. It does not take into account the house payback (return percentage) since it is only tracking the number of bets multiplied by the size of the bet. Keep in mind that this chart is only an approximation and that every individual's speed is different.

You see by the chart that the fewer coins played per pull, the longer it takes to reach the level shown. Similarly, the slower the player's average playing speed, the longer it will take.

Since the average player will play the full number of coins allowed by the machine, and the experienced player tends to go at faster paces, you can expect that the action levels will be hit more often at the faster pace.

ACTION CHART - $5,000

Coin	Coins Played	Speed of Play	
		Fast	Slow
5¢	5	50 hours	56 hours
	3	81 hours	94 hours
	1	250 hours	300 hours
25¢	5	10 hours	11.5 hours
	3	16.5 hours	19 hours
	1	50 hours	60 hours
$1	5	2.5 hour	4 hours
	3	4 hours	5 hours
	1	12.5 hours	15 hours
$5	5	30 minutes	35 minutes
	3	46 minutes	55 minutes
	1	2.5 hours	3 hours

This chart shows approximately how long it would take to reach **$5,000** in action. It does not take into account the house payback (return percentage) since it is only tracking the number of bets multiplied by the size of the bet. Keep in mind that this chart is only an approximation and that every individual's speed is different.

You see by the chart that the fewer coins played per pull, the longer it takes to reach the level shown. Similarly, the slower the player's average playing speed, the longer it will take.

Since the average player will play the full number of coins allowed by the machine, and the experienced player tends to go at faster paces, you can expect that the action levels will be hit more often at the faster pace.

ACTION CHART - $10,000

Coin	Coins Played	Speed of Play	
		Fast	Slow
5¢	5	100 hours	115 hours
	3	165 hours	190 hours
	1	500 hours	600 hours
25¢	5	20 hours	23 hours
	3	33 hours	38 hours
	1	100 hours	120 hours
$1	5	5 hours	7.5 hours
	3	7.5 hours	10 hours
	1	25 hours	30 hours
$5	5	1 hour	1.25 hours
	3	1.5 hours	2 hours
	1	5 hours	6.25 hours

This chart shows approximately how long it would take to reach **$10,000** in action. It does not take into account the house payback (return percentage) since it is only tracking the number of bets multiplied by the size of the bet. Keep in mind that this chart is only an approximation and that every individual's speed is different.

You see by the chart that the fewer coins played per pull, the longer it takes to reach the level shown. Similarly, the slower the player's average playing speed, the longer it will take.

Since the average player will play the full number of coins allowed by the machine, and the experienced player tends to go at faster paces, you can expect that the action levels will be hit more often at the faster pace.

SLOTS CLUBS

PLANNING AHEAD

Remember to prepare for your next trip to Las Vegas or wherever you might be gambling by contacting, in advance, the slots clubs at the casinos where you might be playing. Get yourself set up in advance. Most casinos have toll-free numbers, and they would be glad to give you the information.

Of course, you can always sign up when you arrive, and that's no problem. But if you alert a casino that you're coming, you might just get it to send you incentives and comp tickets in advance to make sure you visit and play.

17. JACKPOTS & TAXES

Before we go any further in this chapter, let me alert you that I am not an accountant, nor a lawyer, and I am no expert in tax law either. If indeed you win a jackpot, you will be best served if you hire competent help to determine the proper reporting of gambling income and deductions to the IRS or other tax body. In other words, while off on your jackpot vacation, don't use me as the final source. Peel off a bill or two and give it to the pros. Below I've provided some general guidelines as I understand them.

Casinos are required by law to ensure that any single slot type machine payout of $1,200 and over is reported to the Internal Revenue Service. A form called a W-2G must immediately be completed by the $1,200 winner at the casino so that it can be forwarded to the IRS.

The W-2G form is comparable to the W-2 form you receive from your employer. The W-2 verifies the amount of money you have made in any given period of time, while the W-2G validates the money you received in slot machine winnings. The total dollar amount on the W-2G is added to your earnings on your W-2 form to determine your total taxable income for the year.

SECRETS OF WINNING VIDEO POKER

For example, if your annual household income is $30,000 and you won $2,000 playing video poker, your total taxable income for the year would increase to $32,000.

You must make two valid forms of identification available to the casino at the time of any win. These might include a driver's license, credit card or social security card.

The government allows slot and video poker machine gamblers to deduct losses up to but not exceeding the amount they won. If, for example, if you won a $2,000 jackpot in one year playing the slots but lost a miscellaneous total of $2,500 in that same year, you would not be able to take the $500 difference as a loss off your taxes.

The losses to be offset against winnings can't be subtracted directly from the itemized winnings. They must be taken separately as a miscellaneous deduction. This way the government is able to see exact winnings and exact losses. Losses from the previous year will not be accepted as losses for the present year. For example, if that $2,500 loss had come from the previous year's play, you would be unable to deduct it against the current year's $2,000 win.

If you win a jackpot under $1,200, the casino is not required to report your winnings.

KEEPING LOGBOOKS

If you're a serious player, it is important to keep itemized logs of daily amounts lost and won at the slot machines so that if you do win a jackpot, you can offset the jackpot total against all the losses it took to get you there. Dates, times and places are important to include in these journals. Keeping the names of any employees or witnesses who are able to verify your losses may be helpful. All of this may seem tedious, but when you're forced to deal with the Internal Revenue Service, your records can never be too detailed.

A simple way to tally daily wins and losses is to carry a small notebook, diary or journal. This will make it easy for you to jot down information as you play. If someone is playing with you, both of you may want to take turns recording necessary information. All transactions should be accounted for during or after each gambling session. The more verification you have of loss deductions, the more substantial and acceptable your loss claims will be.

Even if you're playing only casually, it may be wise to keep at least an informal record. You never know when you might hit the jackpot. A record will also let you know, in black and white, how you have done at the machines.

Sometimes the IRS demands additional evidence for gambling losses. These might include airline tickets, hotel bills, gas receipts or signed documents from witnesses who are able to verify your losses. Witnesses could be other players, the change person, slots host or casino supervisor. All of the time put into this documentation process will be well worth it if you do hit some sweet ones.

Slots club players may also get loss documentation from the casinos. Their sophisticated tracking systems keep tally of everything – hours played, amount of coins bet, wins and losses, coin denominations – all for the purpose of tracking your action and giving you comps for your good play. If you nail a jackpot or two, this documentation is indisputable evidence for your claims.

Let me remind you again that you will need to seek competent tax advice from a professional if you should hit some big wins, and especially if you hit a monster jackpot. This isn't the worst worry in the world to have – needing to figure out all the ways to minimize your tax burden from a multimillion dollar jackpot. You'd best take it easy on a tropical beach for a few months before you tackle the serious implications of that one.

18. MONEY MANAGEMENT & WINNING

The first step toward being a winning player is managing your money. It does you no good to hit a hot streak and quickly pile up several hundred dollars in winnings, if you only lose it all (and that much more).

The player who consistently gives his or her winnings back to the casino is a player who doesn't give himself or herself a chance to win. In a sense, that's a player who *refuses* to win. No matter how well a session is going, the player feels the need to keep playing until the money is gone. This player I describe is a loser, not a winner. Only an unusually long winning streak or a monster jackpot can put this player in the win column. This type of player plays as if the goal is to lose. And if he or she can't lose it today, there is always tomorrow. If you're a player hell-bent on losing, it doesn't take long for the odds to catch up.

But losing is not what this book is about. It's about winning, and that's what I want you to concentrate on. What I'm trying to teach you here is how to win. Part of this formula is using the winning techniques and strategies I describe throughout this book. Another part – the most important part – is money management. If you don't handle your money intelligently and with a good plan from the start, you're going to be a loser at gambling.

Money management has several aspects to it:

FIVE MONEY MANAGEMENT PRINCIPLES

First and foremost is having a *winning attitude*. To be a winner, you have to *really want to be a winner*.

Second, you must *play within your means*. We'll discuss bankroll considerations and optimal bet size for your bankroll here. We'll also continue this discussion in setting loss limits.

Third is the importance of, *protecting your winning streaks*. We've talked a lot about restricting your losses, and this section shows you how to keep the wins. There are some basic principles that you must always follow.

Fourth, you must have *emotional control*. You must be able to control yourself at the machines and not let yourself be overwhelmed by the gambling atmosphere and your emotions.

Fifth and finally, you must *set limits*. You can never allow yourself to take such a beating at the machines that not only does your vacation get ruined, but you also lose more money than you can afford to lose. Any time that happens, it's always a disaster.

MONEY MANAGEMENT & WINNING

Let's look at each of these money management elements in turn. We'll begin with the winning attitude.

1. THE WINNING ATTITUDE

I am continually amazed at the number of players who always manage to lose during their trips to Las Vegas, Atlantic City, the riverboats, Indian reservations, the Bahamas, and all the other gambling meccas around the world. And it's not just video poker players. I see blackjack and craps players, poker players, slots and roulette players – basically, gamblers of all stripes – consistently losing because they don't come into the casino with a winning attitude.

Does a good attitude affect the odds of the games or the machines? No. Whether you're the happiest camper on Earth (and worry about nothing besides your lollipop flavor) or the sorriest loser this side of suckersville, the odds are the same. The slot machines won't care how you feel, because they won't know. And the odds on those machines aren't affected either. If you and I sit down to pull the handle for ten spins each, it won't matter which one of us pushes the button and sets the reels in motion. The result will be the same, regardless of our moods or what our horoscopes say.

But how you feel most definitely affects your overall chances of winning – there's no two ways about it. A player who goes into the casino with the goal of winning does everything he or she can do to achieve that goal. This gambler will closely follow the money management advice I lay down in this section. That's the mark of a winner. He'll play within his means, he'll set reasonable limits, he'll control himself at the machines, and when he's winning big, the casinos will see his back at the cashier's cage converting the loot into bills before they see that money again.

Losers, on the other hand, will do everything wrong. From the outside, to the casual observer, they will appear as if their goal is to lose. Losers have *loser* written all over them – in their actions, their moods, and of course, their results. No crowbar will pry these players away from the machines or tables until they've managed to lose their money. We've all seen plenty of these players. Me, I've seen and heard enough stories to fill an encyclopedia of gambler's stories about losers.

To be sure, the casinos hold the edge at certain machines, and in many places the edge is substantial. But players can still beat unfavorable machines (and they can beat ones where they have the edge as well). That is, the *smart* players can. Follow the advice in this section, and you'll be smart, too – the one gambler the casinos don't feast on. You'll feast on them instead.

The next stop in money management is figuring out the correct bankroll for *you* and playing within those limits.

2. BANKROLLING:
PLAY WITHIN YOUR MEANS

Determining the correct bankroll for you as a player is not just about the money you can afford to risk at the machines from a financial point of view, it's also about what you can afford to lose emotionally. You must never gamble at a level that exceeds what you can afford, and that goes for financially as well as emotionally. There is no more important rule in all of gambling than this one.

The possibilities of taking a loss are real, and if that loss will hurt, you're playing like a fool. It is inevitable that players who gamble over their heads will lose more than they can afford. Luck won't help these players because even when the good music comes their way, as it surely will, they won't quit winners. They must keep on going and going and going until the inevitable occurs. It is almost axiomatic that the player who bets too much is going to lose.

By definition, the player who loses when he or she bets too much is getting hurt. Don't let that player be you. Gambling with needed funds is foolish. However, if you never play over your head, you'll never suffer.

Luck fluctuates in gambling. Sometimes you win, sometimes you lose. Every player knows that. The goal for intelligent gamblers is to protect themselves in the times they lose, and that means to set loss limits not only for a particular session, but for an entire trip as well.

Let's go over some basic bankrolling principles.

Session Bankroll

You want to bring enough money to the machines so you can handle a moderate losing streak, but still have enough playing stake money so that luck can turn itself around and maybe swing the fortune in the other direction. That amount, which we'll get to in a second, will be your one session stake. If that stake gets drained, then you call it a day.

The key concept in formulating single session bankrolls for a machine is to restrict losses to affordable amounts. That's why when I discuss bringing money to a machine, I say to bring "moderate" amounts, not substantial amounts. *Minimizing* losses is the key. You can't always win. That's a fact of life for gamblers. If you're losing, keep the losses affordable – take a break. Don't let yourself get caught in a situation where you get beat badly. There's always another day.

You should have enough money at the machines to cover about sixty plays. A **play** is the amount of money you'll be betting on one spin. For example, if you're playing 25¢ machines and are playing five coins at a time, your play costs $1.25. Thus, your bankroll for the session should be about $75. If your coin instead was $1, then you would need a $300 stake (60 plays x $5). 5¢ players should bring $15 at five coins per spin. These are the maximum numbers. You can risk less, which you might want to do anyway.

These conservative numbers are designed to keep your losses to affordable amounts. This doesn't mean that you'll lose the amounts shown above, only that *you won't lose more than that*. That's a big step in the right direction right there.

Trip Bankroll
A trip to a casino is really a multitude of individual sessions. For short trips, like a weekend jaunt, you want to have enough to cover three sessions, for longer trips, say up to a week or two, four to five sessions. The purpose of the trip bankroll is to have enough money to keep you playing, even though you may be having a particularly bad run of

luck, but at the same time to restrict your overall losses to "acceptable" amounts.

That's why we take such a conservative approach. By avoiding overbetting, you give yourself the opportunity to bounce back after bad luck. You also avoid getting wiped out or, even worse, digging deeper in your pockets and getting destroyed.

Thus, using the figures we worked out above with five coins average per play, 25¢ players should bring $225 for a weekend, $1 players should bring $900, and 5¢ players should bring $45. These bankroll amounts allow you to withstand any normal losing streak and still have the resources to play more and bounce back to come out on top. If the numbers scare you, then you need to think about lower denomination machines. Money can be lost at the machines, and you probably know that as well as I do. It's better to play it safe.

3. PROTECT YOUR WINNING STREAKS

Once you've accumulated a sizable win at the video poker machines and had yourself a good run, the most important thing is to walk away a winner. There is no worse feeling than skulking away from a machine after having lost all your winnings.

The general guideline I recommend is to put away three-fourths or more of your winnings into a "protected" area that you won't touch under any circumstances. That money is bankable – you won't play it. Whether those wins are put aside as coins in a "no touch zone" plastic bucket, as a mental note to shut off after you drop to a certain number of credits, or in any other way, *make sure you do it.*

Never touch the money you've set aside in your protected zone. Never. Protecting your wins is just as important as limiting your losses. Once the coins or credits are on your side, it's your money, not the casino's. It's yours now. You risked and you won. Great. Now take it home with you and do something fun with it.

For example, let's say you're up $200 after a pretty good session at the $1 machines. Put $150 of that money into your protected zone. Play out the $50. This doesn't mean you have to lose the $50. If things turn sour, you can call it quits at $25, and now guarantee yourself an extra $25 win! But, in any case, don't dip below the $50. If that buffer is gone, you're gone – a winner.

Keep playing with the remaining quarter of your winnings, putting more aside as the wins accumulate. If you do this, your guaranteed winning pile steadily increases. Ride the cycle upwards. If the $200 mushrooms to $350, now move the extra $100 to your winnings and play again with the left-over $50. If your bankroll still increases with more wins, put more aside again.

Once the winning streak stops and the tides of fortune turn against you, it's time to leave the machines. You're now a guaranteed winner who, later on, looks back on that profitable session with great satisfaction.

Set no limits on a winning streak. When you've got a hot

hand, ride it for all it's worth. And when things cool down, chill out with a cool one down by the music lounge.

4. EMOTIONAL CONTROL

Astute gamblers have one thing in common – they know how to manage their money and keep cool in the thick of the casino, whether they're up and riding high or struggling against a cold machine with the worst of luck. Superior playing skills alone do not make one a winning player. The concept here is self control, a player's ability to keep the game in check while never losing sight of the winning strategies.

Winning and losing streaks are a very real part of playing video poker. It is how a player deals with the inherent ups and downs that determines just how well he or she will fare overall. We're all going to lose sometimes and we're also going to win sometimes, as well. But it is the smart gambler, however, the one keeping it all under control, that will win when he's winning, and minimize losses when he's losing. It's all about emotional control. We can't change the spins on the reel. We can, however, change our reactions to them.

Let's show a simple example of how loss of emotional control can quickly change a big winning session into a disaster. Let's say a bettor starts out with a bankroll of $200 and has been playing 25¢ machines. After two hours of play, he has ridden a surge of luck to $225 in winnings. Now he has $425 in front of him.

Getting greedy and caught up in the excitement of the

game, the gambler now really wants to put the squeeze on and fast, so he goes against his pre-planned strategy, if he even has one, and now goes for the $1 machines. With a little luck and a few big wins in a row, he's on easy street.

However, after a bunch of losses, he gets frantic. He goes for two machines at a time, pushing all his money out there. And now, more bad luck. Suddenly, a careful strategy that netted $225 morphed into an "if I can get lucky on this play, please" strategy. No surprise – the player loses all the money. Madness. He lost control, bet over his head, took what by all rights was a tremendous winning session and finished just a short time later with nothing!

5. SETTING LIMITS

This is really a continuation of our discussion on bankrolling, but then again, when the discussion concerns some aspect of money management, everything is related. You always want to set a limit on losses so that one bad session doesn't devastate you. At the same time, you should set a stop-loss on winnings, as well, so that once you have a good win going, you never give the casino a chance to get the money back.

Before sitting at the table and making your bets, you must decide on the amount of money you'll put at stake, and should luck turn against you, restrict your losses to that amount only. If you don't go against this rule, you can never take a big beating. If things go poorly at first, take a break – simple as that.

When you're winning big, put a good chunk of these winnings in a "don't touch" pile and play with the rest. You never want to hand all your winnings back to the casino. Should a losing streak occur, you're out of there – a winner!!!

Never risk needed money at the machines no matter how lucky you feel. Just as many "lucky" players contributed to the phenomenal growth of casinos as did the unlucky players. Well, perhaps there are lots more of the latter, but you get the point. The reality of gambling is that money can be lost, and if that money is earmarked for rent or food or any other necessity in your life, you're making a whopping mistake.

I know this is all common sense, but it bears repeating because so many players go against this basic rule. There's an old Las Vegas saying about a guy who rides into town in a $20,000 Cadillac and leaves in a $100,000 Greyhound bus. Unfortunately, that saying bears a lot of truth. The list of sad stories from out of control gamblers can stack a pile of papers up to the thin air of the cerulean sky. And more are added every day, lots more.

Let's say you're a quarter player on a winning streak that has expanded your starting machine bankroll for the day from $100 to $350. That's a nice $250 win. Should you go up to the $1 machine to really go for the kill? Absolutely not. You're hot and you're winning. The action is good. But raising your stake to the $1 machines now magnifies all the bets. Sure you can win a lot more. But don't let greed lead you astray. Greed nabs most gamblers, and the end result every time is an unhappy player who got buried by that greed.

All that's needed for the winds of fortune to change is a short losing streak at a higher level. That will wipe out *all* your winnings, and perhaps, since greed has overcome your sanity, dig you into a deep ditch quickly. Not good. You cannot afford to be playing at a level that spells danger, and betting over your head spells danger.

So many gamblers do this that I always wonder at their goals. Are they really trying to win, or are they raising the stakes so the fall is bigger? They'll win say $300, bump up the stakes, and if they don't get wiped out at the higher level, they bump up the stakes one more time. Well, it catches up quickly. Eventually, luck will turn, it always does. If these players were smart, they would get out while the getting was good. But inevitably, and almost invariably, they will not leave until they take the big fall.

What are these players really trying to do? The psychology on all this is complex, but the empirical evidence is always the same. They lose it all back and more. There is almost no way that these gamblers can come out ahead. No matter how lucky they get, they raise the stakes again so that all it takes is a small losing streak to wipe it all out – their winnings, their original stake, and then, in their desperation, even more. I've seen it time and time again. And then these players wonder, "What happened?"

Greed happened, baby, and a loss of control. But we can make this all easy right now. Stick to the level at which you started, so that when you do win, you stay a winner. It's okay to reach for the stars, but don't be jumping off the bridge to catch them. Whether you win or lose at video poker, always stick to the level of betting that you originally picked.

REMEMBER: YOU'RE PLAYING FOR FUN

Gambling is a form of entertainment. If you can't afford the possibility of losing, don't gamble at the stakes you were considering. Either play at lower levels or don't gamble at all. If the playing of the game becomes a cause for undue anxiety, for whatever the reason, then it ceases to be a form of entertainment, and you need a break. Take some time away from the game – be it a coffee break or a month's rest.

Playing under anxiety not only ruins the fun of the game but also adversely affects play. It can influence you to make decisions contrary to what smart strategy dictates. Your goal in gambling is not just to win, but also to get satisfaction out of the game. Keep that in mind and you can never go wrong.

You can't always win – even when the odds favor you – and you won't always lose, even when the odds are against you. In the short run, anything can happen, and it usually does. But over the long run, luck evens itself out. It is skill, in the bets you make and how you play the game, that will determine if you are a winner or a loser.

19. A FINAL WORD

Well, that's about it. I've covered a lot of material in this book. Hopefully, I've given you a good shot at beating video poker machines. Good luck, and practice your skill!

Avery Cardoza

GLOSSARY

Action - The total amount of money played measured by the sum of all bets placed. Thus, betting a quarter 100 times, would be equivalent to $25.00 in *action*, and betting $1 for 700 plays adds up to $700 in *action*. Action does not take into account starting or ending bankroll, nor wins or losses – just total amount of bets.

Bank, Bank of Machines - This is a group of machines connected together in a structure as a design unit.

Big Coin Machine - A video machine requiring $5 or $25 coins to play.

Big Coin Player - A player who plays $5 or $25 coins.

Bonus Quads - A Jacks or Better machine that offers special bonus payouts on specified four of a kind hands.

Bonus Royal - Type of video poker machine that gives a large bonus payout on a specified royal flush if you hit it.

Cage - The cashier's cage, where players can exchange chips for cash or change traveler's checks. The cage usually won't accept large numbers of coins. They must be exchanged at a change booth.

Change Booth - A booth set up for the specific purpose of changing players' bills into coins or their coins into bills.

Changeperson - The casino employee who services the machines area for the purpose of changing bills into coins.

Cashout Button - This button, when pressed, releases all the coins that were won and held by the machine.

Changeperson - The casino employee responsible for changing players' bills into coins. The changeperson usually roams the slots area, though he or she may be "stationed" in a carousel.

Cold - A machine that is paying out less than expected, or a player on a losing streak.

Comp - Short for *complimentary*. The freebies given out by the casino, usually as a reward for play. These can take the form of free or discounted drinks, rooms, shows, buffets and regular meals, and more.

Credits - The number of coins that a player has on "credit" in the machine which can be used for future play. Credits are accumulated through winnings or when money is inserted into the machine.

GLOSSARY

Deal/Draw Button - This button, when pressed, deals the cards.

Denomination - The size of coin (or bill) used to play a particular machine. The 25¢ and $1 machines are the most popular denominations found. Increasingly, larger denominations such as $5, $25, $100, and even higher are found as well.

Deuces Wild - A video poker variation where all deuces are wild cards, that is, they can be used as any card that would most benefit the player, even though that card may already be used.

Deuces and Joker Wild - A video poker game dealt from a 53 card deck, the regular 52 card deck plus a wild joker. All deuces are wild in this game too, for five wild cards.

Discard - A card that a player chooses not to keep, instead drawing a new one.

Double Card Option - This feature, found on some video poker machines, uses a 53rd card deck to deal the game. The 53rd card is actually an extra card, a double of one of the other cards in the deck, and when this card is received in a player's hand, the payout is doubled. Though seemingly attractive, this feature is disadvantageous for the player.

Double Down Stud - A video poker variation that deals four cards and gives players the option either to double their bet and receive the fifth card, or to fold and give up their bet.

Draw - To take cards as a replacement for discarded ones.

Double or Nothing Button - A feature on some machines that allows winning hands to double their bet at the risk of losing it all in a one card showdown draw, high card wins, against the machine.

Five-of-a-kind - A hand containing five cards of the same rank, for example, 4 4 4 4 2 (where the 2 is used as a wild card).

Five Deck Frenzy - The Progressive variation of Five Deck Poker.

Five Deck Poker - This video poker variation assigns one deck of cards to each video poker position so that in theory, a player could hold five cards of the same suit and value.

Flush - Five cards of the same suit. The hand 3 7 8 J K of spades would be a spade flush.

Full House - A hand containing three cards of the same value (three-of-a-kind) and two cards of another identical value (a pair). Q Q Q K K would be a full house.

Full Pay - Machines with the best basic payout schedules found for their type.

GLOSSARY

Hand - The player's five cards.

High Card - In Jacks or Better, a jack, queen, king, and ace. In 10s or Better, the 10 as well.

High Roller Machine - A video machine requiring $100 or $500 coins to play.

High Roller - A video poker player who plays $100 or $500 coins.

Hold - The action of keeping a card, not discarding it, or the button marked as such which is used for this purpose. Also, the percentage or actual dollar amounts a casino wins from its players. Also known as **Hold Percentage.**

Hold Button - The button that, when pressed, tells the machine to keep the card. When it is pressed again, it releases the "hold" and tells the machine to discard the card.

Inside Straight - A four-card straight that can only be filled in the middle, not on either end. For example, 5 6 8 9 is an inside straight since only a 7 will fill it.

Jackpot - A very big winner. Hitting the royal flush is hitting a jackpot.

Jacks or Better - The standard video poker machine that pays out for any poker hand of at least jacks or higher. Also, refers to a hand of at least the strength of jacks, that is, jacks, queens, kings, or aces, or any higher combination.

Joker Wild - A video poker machine dealt from a 53-card deck, the regular 52-card deck plus a joker which serves as a wild card.

Long Run - The concept of what certain results are expected to be when occurring over many trials, thus *in the long run.*

Low Pair - A pair that doesn't qualify for a payout. In Jacks or Better, that would be a hand of 10s or worse.

Max Bet Button - See **Max Coin Button**.

Max Coin Button - The button that plays all credits allowed (usually five) when it's pushed.

Medium Coin Machine - A $1 machine.

Medium Coin Player - A player who plays the $1 machines.

Mega-Progressive Machines - A progressive video poker machine with an enormous, usually million dollar, jackpot.

Money Management - The strategy used by smart players to preserve their capital, avoid big losses, and manage their wins.

GLOSSARY

Multiple Progressives - A machine which contains more than one progressive jackpot.

One Credit Button - The button that plays one credit for the player when pushed. The deal button will need to be pushed after to deal the cards.

Pair - Two cards of the same value, such as two 5s or two jacks.

Payback or Payout Percentage - The expected return percentage for money wagered. A 97% payback states that the expected return on every dollar bet will be 97¢, for a loss of 3¢.

Paytable - The display on the video poker machine showing winning combinations and their payouts.

Payout Meter - The display on the machine that shows the number of coins played and won on a spin.

Pokermania - The progressive video poker game linked to the Atlantic City casinos.

Progressive Machines, Progressives - Progressives feature a growing jackpot that increases each time a coin is inserted into a machine that is hooked up to the progressive meter. When the winning combination does hit, usually a Royal Flush, the lucky player wins the total accumulated and posted in the display, and the jackpot total will be reset to a predetermined starting point.

Quad - A specified four-of-a-kind hand that pays a bonus amount if drawn.

Rating - The evaluation received by a player from the casino stating the level of action this player gives the casino.

Royal Flush - The A K Q J 10, all of the same suit.

Second Chance - Video poker feature, sometimes found, that allows players to receive a sixth card in an additional "second draw" if the drawing of that one card would give the player a chance to make a straight or better hand.

Sequential Royal Flush - Refers to a royal flush that must be hit in an exact order by position. For example, the royal may need to be in order with the 10 being in the leftmost position, then consecutively, the jack, queen, king, and finally the ace in the rightmost position.

Short Pay - Machines with less than the best basic payout schedules found for their type. Short pay machines give the house a larger advantage than the better paying full pays preferred by savvy players.

Short Run - A brief sequence of trials, where anything can happen, even though the odds say they may not.

Slots Club - A casino club set up to reward frequent slots and video poker players with comps and rewards.

Slots Host - The casino employee responsible for taking care of the slots and video poker players.

GLOSSARY

Small Coin Machine - A 5¢ or 25¢ machine.

Small Coin Player - A player who plays the 5¢, 10¢, or 25¢ denomination machines.

Straight - Five consecutive non-suited cards, such as an 8 9 10 J Q. If the cards were all of the same suit, then the hand would be a straight flush (next). If an ace is contained in a straight, it must be either the highest or the lowest card of the sequence, or the hand is not a straight. Q K A 2 3 is not a straight.

Straight Flush - Five consecutive cards all in the same suit, for example, the 4 5 6 7 8 of clubs.

Suit - One of the following groups: hearts, diamonds, spades, and clubs.

Tens or Better - A video poker variation that pays out for any poker hand of at least tens or higher.

Three-of-a-kind - Three cards of the same value, such as 9 9 9. Also called **trips**.

Triple Play - An interesting video poker variation that features the simultaneous play of three poker hands.

Trips - See **three of a kind**.

Two Pair - A five card hand that contains two sets of identically valued cards (two pairs) such as 7 7 A A.

SECRETS OF WINNING VIDEO POKER

Two Pairs or Better - A video poker variation that requires a minimum hand of two pairs for a payout.

Well - The bottom metal area of the machine where winning coins fall.

Wild - Any card that is designated as a wild card (see below).

Wild Card - Cards designated as "wild" can be given any value or suit, even as a duplicate or triplicate of a card already held.

GREAT POKER BOOKS
ADD THESE TO YOUR LIBRARY - ORDER NOW!

TOURNAMENT POKER by Tom McEvoy - Rated by pros as best book on tournaments ever written, and enthusiastically endorsed by more than 5 world champions, this is a must for every player's library. Packed solid with winning strategies for all 11 games in the World Series of Poker, with extensive discussions of 7-card stud, limit hold'em, pot and no-limit hold'em, Omaha high-low, re-buy, half-half tournaments, satellites, strategies for each stage of tournaments. Big player profiles. 344 pages, paperback, $39.95.

OMAHA HI-LO POKER by Shane Smith - Learn essential winning strategies for beating Omaha high-low; the best starting hands, how to play the flop, turn, and river, how to read the board for both high and low, dangerous draws, and how to win low-limit tournaments. Smith shows the differences between Omaha high-low and hold'em strategies. Includes odds charts, glossary, low-limit tips, strategic ideas. 84 pages, 8 x 11, spiral bound, $17.95.

7-CARD STUD (THE COMPLETE COURSE IN WINNING AT MEDIUM & LOWER LIMITS) by Roy West - Learn the latest strategies for winning at $1-$4 spread-limit up to $10-$20 fixed-limit games. Covers starting hands, 3rd-7th street strategy for playing most hands, overcards, selective aggressiveness, reading hands, secrets of the pros, psychology, more - in a 42 "lesson" informal format. Includes bonus chapter on 7-stud tournament strategy by World Champion Tom McEvoy. 160 pages, paperback, $24.95.

POKER TOURNAMENT TIPS FROM THE PROS by Shane Smith - Essential advice from poker theorists, authors, and tournament winners on the best strategies for winning the big prizes at low-limit re-buy tournaments. Learn the best strategies for each of the four stages of play–opening, middle, late and final–how to avoid 26 potential traps, advice on re-buys, aggressive play, clock-watching, inside moves, top 20 tips for winning tournaments, more. Advice from McEvoy, Caro, Malmuth, Ciaffone, others. 144 pages, paperback, $19.95.

WINNING LOW LIMIT HOLD'EM by Lee Jones - This essential book on playing 1-4, 3-6, and 1-4-8-8 low limit hold'em is packed with insights on winning: pre-flop positional play; playing the flop in all positions with a pair, two pair, trips, overcards, draws, made and nothing hands; turn and river play; how to read the board; avoiding trash hands; using the check-raise; bluffing, stereotypes, much more. Includes quizzes with answers. Terrific book. 176 pages, 5 1/2 x 8 1/2, paperback, $19.95.

WINNING POKER FOR THE SERIOUS PLAYER by Edwin Silberstang - New edition! More than 100 actual examples provide tons of advice on beating 7 Card Stud, Texas Hold 'Em, Draw Poker, Loball, High-Low and more than 10 other variations. Silberstang analyzes the essentials of being a great player; reading tells, analyzing tables, playing position, mastering the art of deception, creating fear at the table. Also, psychological tactics, when to play aggressive or slow play, or fold, expert plays, more. Colorful glossary included. 288 pages, 6 x 9, perfect bound, $16.95.

WINNER'S GUIDE TO TEXAS HOLD 'EM POKER by Ken Warren - This comprehensive book on beating hold 'em shows serious players how to play every hand from every position with every type of flop. Learn the 14 categories of starting hands, the 10 most common hold 'em tells, how to evaluate a game for profit, and more! Over 50,000 copies in print. 256 pages, 5 1/2 x 8 1/2, paperback, $14.95.

KEN WARREN TEACHES TEXAS HOLD 'EM by Ken Warren - In 33 comprehensive yet easy-to-read chapters, you'll learn absolutely everything about the great game of Texas hold 'em poker. You'll learn to play from every position, at every stage of a hand. You'll master a simple but thorough system for keeping records and understanding odds. And you'll gain expert advice on raising, stealing blinds, avoiding tells, playing for jackpots, bluffing, tournament play, and much more. 416 pages, 6 x 9, $24.95.

THE CHAMPIONSHIP BOOKS
POWERFUL BOOKS YOU MUST HAVE

CHAMPIONSHIP OMAHA (Omaha High-Low, Pot-limit Omaha, Limit High Omaha) by T. J. Cloutier & Tom McEvoy. Clearly-written strategies and powerful advice from Cloutier and McEvoy who have won four World Series of Poker titles in Omaha tournaments. Powerful advice shows you how to win at low-limit and high-stakes games, how to play against loose and tight opponents, and the differing strategies for rebuy and freezeout tournaments. Learn the best starting hands, when slowplaying a big hand is dangerous, what danglers are and why winners don't play them, why pot-limit Omaha is the only poker game where you sometimes fold the nuts on the flop and are correct in doing so and overall, how can you win a lot of money at Omaha! 230 pages, photos, illustrations, $39.95.

CHAMPIONSHIP STUD (Seven-Card Stud, Stud 8/or Better and Razz) by Dr. Max Stern, Linda Johnson, and Tom McEvoy. The authors, who have earned millions of dollars in major tournaments and cash games, eight World Series of Poker bracelets and hundreds of other titles in competition against the best players in the world show you the winning strategies for medium-limit side games as well as poker tournaments and a general tournament strategy that is applicable to any form of poker. Includes give-and-take conversations between the authors to give you more than one point of view on how to play poker. 200 pages, hand pictorials, photos. $29.95.

CHAMPIONSHIP HOLD'EM by T. J. Cloutier & Tom McEvoy. Hard-hitting hold'em the way it's played today in both limit cash games and tournaments. Get killer advice on how to win more money in rammin'-jammin' games, kill-pot, jackpot, shorthanded, and other types of cash games. You'll learn the thinking process before the flop, on the flop, on the turn, and at the river with specific suggestions for what to do when good or bad things happen plus 20 illustrated hands with play-by-play analyses. Specific advice for rocks in tight games, weaklings in loose games, experts in solid games, how hand values change in jackpot games, when you should fold, check, raise, reraise, check-raise, slowplay, bluff, and tournament strategies for small buy-in, big buy-in, rebuy, incremental add-on, satellite and big-field major tournaments. Wow! Easy-to-read and conversational, if you want to become a lifelong winner at limit hold'em, you need this book! 320 Pages, Illustrated, Photos. $39.95

CHAMPIONSHIP NO-LIMIT & POT LIMIT HOLD'EM by T. J. Cloutier & Tom McEvoy The definitive guide to winning at two of the world's most exciting poker games! Written by eight time World Champion players T. J. Cloutier (1998 Player of the Year) and Tom McEvoy (the foremost author on tournament strategy) who have won millions of dollars playing no-limit and pot-limit hold'em in cash games and major tournaments around the world. You'll get all the answers here - no holds barred - to your most important questions: How do you get inside your opponents' heads and learn how to beat them at their own game? How can you tell how much to bet, raise, and reraise in no-limit hold'em? When can you bluff? How do you set up your opponents in pot-limit hold'em so that you can win a monster pot? What are the best strategies for winning no-limit and pot-limit tournaments, satellites, and supersatellites? You get rock-solid and inspired advice from two of the most recognizable figures in poker — advice that you can bank on. If you want to become a winning player, a champion, you must have this book. 209 pages, paperback, illustrations, photos. $39.95

Order Toll-Free 1-800-577-WINS or use order form on page 191

POWERFUL POKER SIMULATIONS
A MUST FOR SERIOUS PLAYERS WITH A COMPUTER!
IBM compatibles CD ROM Windows 3.1, 95, and 98 - Full Color Graphics

Play interactive poker against these **incredible** full color poker simulation programs - they're the absolute **best** method to improve game. Computer players act like real players. All games let you set the limits and rake, have fully programmable players, adjustable lineup, stat tracking, and Hand Analyzer for starting hands. MIke Caro, the world's foremost poker theoretician says, "Amazing...A steal for under $500." Includes free telephone support. **New Feature!** - "Smart advisor" gives expert advice for every play in every game!

1. TURBO TEXAS HOLD'EM FOR WINDOWS - $89.95 - Choose which players, how many, 2-10, you want to play, create loose/tight game, control check-raising, bluffing, position, sensitivity to pot odds, more! Also, instant replay, pop-up odds, Professional Advisor, keeps track of play statistics. Free bonus: Hold'em Hand Analyzer analyzes all 169 pocket hands in detail, their win rates under any conditions you set. Caro says this "hold'em software is the most powerful ever created." Great product!

2. TURBO SEVEN-CARD STUD FOR WINDOWS - $89.95 - Create any conditions of play; choose number of players (2-8), bet amounts, fixed or spread limit, bring-in method, tight/loose conditions, position, reaction to board, number of dead cards, stack deck to create special conditions, instant replay. Terrific stat reporting includes analysis of starting cards, 3-D bar charts, graphs. Play interactively, run high speed simulation to test strategies. Hand Analyzer analyzes starting hands in detail. Wow!

3. TURBO OMAHA HIGH-LOW SPLIT FOR WINDOWS - $89.95 -Specify any playing conditions; betting limits, number of raises, blind structures, button position, aggressiveness/passiveness of opponents, number of players (2-10), types of hands dealt, blinds, position, board reaction, specify flop, turn, river cards! Choose opponents, use provided point count or create your own. Statistical reporting, instant replay, pop-up odds, high speed simulation to test strategies, amazing Hand Analyzer, much more!

4. TURBO OMAHA HIGH FOR WINDOWS - $89.95 - Same features as above, but tailored for the Omaha High-only game. Caro says program is "an electrifying research tool...it can clearly be worth thousands of dollars to any serious player. A must for Omaha High players.

5. TURBO 7 STUD 8 OR BETTER - $89.95 - Brand new with all the features you expect from the Wilson Turbo products: the latest artificial intelligence, instant advice and exact odds, play versus 2-7 opponents, enhanced data charts that can be exported or printed, the ability to fold out of turn and immediately go to the next hand, ability to peek at opponents hand, optional warning mode that warns you if a play disagrees with the advisor, and automatic testing mode that can run up to 50 tests unattended. Challenge tough computer players who vary their styles for a truly great poker game.

---

6. TOURNAMENT TEXAS HOLD'EM - $59.95
Set-up for tournament practice and play, this realistic simulation pits you against celebrity look-alikes. Tons of options let you control tournament size with 10 to 300 entrants, select limits, ante, rake, blind structures, freezeouts, number of rebuys and competition level of opponents - average, tough, or toughest. Pop-up status report shows how you're doing vs. the competition. Save tournaments in progress to play again later. Additional feature allows you to quickly finish a folded hand and go on to the next.

GRI'S PROFESSIONAL VIDEO POKER STRATEGY
Win Money at Video Poker! With the Odds!

At last, for the **first time,** and for **serious players only,** the GRI **Professional Video Poker** strategy is released so you too can play to win! **You read it right** - this strategy gives you the **mathematical advantage** over the casino and what's more, it's **easy to learn!**

PROFESSIONAL STRATEGY SHOWS YOU HOW TO WIN WITH THE ODDS - This **powerhouse strategy,** played for **big profits** by an **exclusive** circle of **professionals,** people who make their living at the machines, is now made available to you! You too can win - with the odds - and this **winning strategy** shows you how!

HOW TO PLAY FOR A PROFIT - You'll learn the **key factors** to play on a **pro level:** which machines will turn you a profit, break-even and win rates, hands per hour and average win per hour charts, time value, team play and more! You'll also learn big play strategy, alternate jackpot play, high and low jackpot play and key strategies to follow.

WINNING STRATEGIES FOR ALL MACHINES - This **comprehensive, advanced pro package** not only shows you how to win money at the 8-5 progressives, but also, the **winning strategies** for 10s or better, deuces wild, joker's wild, flat-top, progressive and special options features.

BE A WINNER IN JUST ONE DAY - **In just one day,** after learning our strategy, you will have the skills to **consistently win money** at video poker - with the odds. The strategies are easy to use under practical casino conditions.

FREE BONUS - PROFESSIONAL PROFIT EXPECTANCY FORMULA ($15 VALUE) - For serious players, we're including this free bonus essay which explains the professional profit expectancy principles of video poker and how to relate them to real dollars and cents in your game.

To order send just $50 by check or money order to:
Cardoza Publishing, P.O. Box 1500, Cooper Station, New York, NY 10276

VIDEOS BY MIKE CARO
THE MAD GENIUS OF POKER

CARO'S PRO POKER TELLS

The long-awaited two-video set is a powerful scientific course on how to use your opponents' gestures, words and body language to read their hands and win all their money. These carefully guarded poker secrets, filmed with 63 poker notables, will revolutionize your game. It reveals when opponents are bluffing, when they aren't, and why. Knowing what your opponent's gestures mean, and protecting them from knowing yours, gives you a huge winning edge. An absolute must buy! $59.95.

CARO'S MAJOR POKER SEMINAR

The legendary "Mad Genius" is at it again, giving poker advice in VHS format. This new tape is based on the inaugural class at Mike Caro University of Poker, Gaming and Life strategy. The material given on this tape is based on many fundamentals introduced in Caro's books, papers, and articles and is prepared in such a way that reinforces concepts old and new. Caro's style is easy-going but intense with key concepts stressed and repeated. This tape will improve your play. 60 Minutes. $24.95.

CARO'S POWER POKER SEMINAR

This powerful video shows you how to win big money using the little-known concepts of world champion players. This advice will be worth thousands of dollars to you every year, even more if you're a big money player! After 15 years of refusing to allow his seminars to be filmed, Caro presents entertaining but serious coverage of his long-guarded secrets. Contains the most profitable poker advice ever put on video. 62 Minutes! $39.95.

Order Toll-Free 1-800-577-WINS or use order form on page 191

CARDOZA PUBLISHING ONLINE

**For the latest in poker, gambling, chess, backgammon, and games
by the world's top authorities and writers**

www.cardozapub.com

To find out about our latest publications and products, to order books and software from third parties, or simply to keep aware of our latest activities in the world or poker, gambling, and other games of chance and skill:

1. Go online: www.cardozapub.com
2. Use E-Mail: cardozapub@aol.com
3. Call toll free: 800-577-WINS (800-577-9467)

BOOKS BY MIKE CARO
THE MAD GENIUS OF POKER

CARO'S BOOK OF TELLS (THE BODY LANGUAGE OF POKER) - Finally! Mike Caro's classic book is now revised and back in print! This long-awaited revision by the Mad Genius of Poker takes a detailed look at the art and science of tells, the physical mannerisms which giveaway a player's hand. Featuring photo illustrations of poker players in action along with Caro's explanations about when players are bluffing and when they're not, these powerful eye-opening ideas can give you the decisive edge at the table! This invaluable book should be in every player's library! 320 pages! $24.95.

CARO'S GUIDE TO DOYLE BRUNSON'S SUPER SYSTEM - Working with World Champion Doyle Brunson, the legendary Mike Caro has created a fresh look to the "Bible" of all poker books, adding new and personal insights that help you understand the original work. Caro breaks 36 concepts into either "Analysis, Commentary, Concept, Mission, Play-By-Play, Psychology, Statistics, Story, or Strategy. Lots of illustrations and winning concepts give even more value to this great work. 86 pages, 8 1/2 x 11, stapled. $19.95.

CARO'S FUNDAMENTAL SECRETS OF WINNING POKER - The world's foremost poker theoretician and strategist presents the essential strategies, concepts, and secret winning plays that comprise the very foundation of winning poker play. Shows how to win more from weak players, equalize stronger players, bluff a bluffer, win big pots, where to sit against weak players, the six factors of strategic table image. Includes selected tips on hold 'em, 7 stud, draw, lowball, tournaments, more. 160 Pages, 5 1/2 x 8 1/2, perfect bound, $12.95.

Call Toll Free (800)577-WINS or Use Coupon Below to Order Books, Videos & Software

BECOME A BETTER POKER PLAYER!

YES! I want to be a winner! Rush me the following items: (Write in choices below):

MAKE CHECKS TO:
Cardoza Publishing
P.O. Box 1500
Cooper Station
New York, NY 10276

CHARGE BY PHONE:
Toll-Free: 1-800-577-WINS
E-Mail Orders: cardozapub@aol.com

Subtotal	
Postage/Handling: First Item	
Additional Postage	
Total Amount Due	

SHIPPING CHARGES: For US orders, include $6.00 postage/handling 1st book ordered; for each additional book, add $1.00. For Canada/Mexico, double above amounts, quadruple (4X) for all other countries. Orders outside U.S., money order payable in U.S. dollars on U.S. bank only.

NAME _____

ADDRESS _____

CITY _____ STATE _____ ZIP _____

30 day money back guarantee!   VidPoker03